# The Black Musical Tradition

AND

# Early Black Literature

# The Black Musical Tradition

*AND*

# Early Black Literature

BY

Robin Walker

REKLAW EDUCATION LTD
London (U.K.)

Copyright © Reklaw Education Limited 2015

All rights reserved. No part of this publication may be reproduced, stored in a retrieval system, or transmitted by any means, without the prior permission in writing from the publisher, nor be otherwise circulated in any form of binding or cover other than that in which it is published and with a similar condition including this condition being imposed on the subsequent purchaser.

## CONTENTS

| | |
|---|---|
| **Opening Remarks** | 1 |
| *PART ONE: THE BLACK MUSICAL TRADITION* | 3 |
| **Introduction** | 5 |
| **Chapter 1: Origins in Africa** | 7 |
| **Chapter 2: Evolution in the Diaspora** | 21 |
| **Chapter 3: From Soul to Grime** | 33 |
| **Notes and References** | 41 |
| *PART TWO: EARLY BLACK LITERATURE* | 45 |
| **Introduction** | 47 |
| **Chapter 1: Egyptian Literature** | 49 |
| **Chapter 2: Negro Arab Literature** | 54 |
| **Chapter 3: Ethiopian Literature** | 59 |
| **Chapter 4: Sudanese Manuscripts** | 65 |
| **Chapter 5: Hausa Literature** | 67 |
| **Chapter 6: Swahili Literature** | 71 |
| **Chapter 7: African American Literature** | 74 |
| **Notes and References** | 85 |

*PART THREE: THE AUTHOR* 91

**Robin Walker** 93
**1. Biography** 93
**2. Speaking Engagements** 94

**Index** 97

## OPENING REMARKS

CAN you be a cultured Black person and know none of the artistic heritage of your people? Can you call yourself a genuinely learned person?

Older people who grew up in the Caribbean were given a colonial British education. They learned to recite whole passages from Tennyson, Keats and Longfellow. My own schooling was a diet of Purcell, Mozart and Beethoven in music. I read mediaeval Scottish ballads, Shakespeare and Taylor Coleridge in literature. In those days, the great Kenneth Clark, through his extraordinary series *Civilisation,* set the benchmark for cultural television showing the visual arts and architecture. Many other television programmes reinforced the cultural importance of crafts, memorabilia and furniture.

Professor Amos Wilson, the great African American psychologist, pointed out that most Black people in the West are culturally divided between two souls. One soul is that of the African that many Black people are (unfortunately) trying to run away from. The other soul is that of the European that many Black people are (unfortunately) trying to run to but actually rejects them. This leads to a mentality of a love hate thing that Black individuals have with themselves, each other, their children and with Europeans. This vacillation is even more pronounced with middle class Blacks. Thus the more education that a person has, the bigger the vacillation appears to be. Put simply, the more a Black person learns about Tennyson, Keats, Longfellow, etcetera, and nothing about their own heritage, the bigger the inferiority complex.

I believe that in an ideal situation, an educated person should learn from ALL heritages. This includes the European, Asian, Australasian, American AND the African heritage. This book, *The Black Musical Tradition and Early Black Literature,* covers two aspects of the African heritage: music and literature. It challenges the idea that Black people were a negligible factor in the development of these intellectual and cultural endeavours.

Part One of the book, *The Black Musical Tradition,* is a critical overview of Black musical heritage from early African times to African American music. I tell the story of the art of sound from the African courts to the Call and the Cries, Blues, Gospel, Jazz, Rock and Roll, Funk, Disco, up to the evolution of Techno.

Part Two of the book, *Early Black Literature,* is an overview of Black writing with translated examples. I tell the story of Ancient Egyptian literature, Negro Arab Literature, Ethiopian literature and African American literature. I also give a survey and an overview of old surviving Sudanese, Hausa and Swahili manuscripts.

Part Three of the book gives information about how to contact me and the lectures that I give on these topics.

Robin Walker

January 2015

# PART ONE

## THE BLACK MUSICAL TRADITION

# INTRODUCTION

MUSIC is an important part of the Black cultural heritage. While it is greatly enjoyed and appreciated, very few Black writers have discussed music from an analytical perspective AS MUSIC. Some will talk about the socio-political-poetic CONTENT OF LYRICS. Others will give biographical information and anecdotes on certain Black musician's LIVES without too much discussion of the music itself. Even fewer, have tried to show COMMONALITIES and traits that run through the different musical forms that connect them to a common tradition or sets of traditions.

In *The Black Musical Tradition,* I place the various types of African and African-derived music into a historical context. I show the links and commonalities that underlie Black Music with a discussion that includes African Court Music, Highlife, Work Song, Blues, Gospel, Ragtime, Jazz, Rhythm & Blues, Reggae, Hip Hop, Techno and House.

This essay is inspired by two exceptional thinkers, Ashenafi Kebede and Albert Murray. Professor Kebede, author of *Roots of Black Music,* tells a coherent story of the origin and evolution of Black music from Africa to America. Mr Murray, author of *Stomping the Blues,* connects the different forms of African American musical genres together by considering the common DNA--The Blues.

In another important source entitled *African and African-American Contributions to World Music* (US, Portland Public Schools, 1989, p.1) Professor C. C. Lawrence-McIntyre explained the importance of Black Music in human culture and the negative commercial pressures exerted on Black musicians: 'In ancient times, the African people of the Nile Valley (particularly Egyptians) led the world in musical development, and that legacy continued with the African people here in the Americas. Music in the African-American Tradition in less than two centuries became the dominant influence on world music. Today we find the Spirituals, Gospel, Blues, Ragtime, the classical form mistakenly labeled "Jazz" and all aspects of African-American music in the movies, on Broadway, on television, in commercial jingles, in music videos, and in untold contemporary uses by people all over the world. The commercial establishments of the modern world reap unimaginable profits from the invention and genius of the transplanted Africans. Through "Soul" music (including Rhythm and Blues/Rock and Roll), Reggae from Jamaica, Salsa from Latin America, and even Highlife from urban African cities, [multinational corporations] exert greater and more powerful social control in the artistic and economic arenas.'

I also draw upon the scholarship of Carl Engel, J. H. Kwabena Nketia, Eileen Southern, and, for the more modern musical forms, a number of television documentaries.

Robin Walker

## CHAPTER 1: ORIGINS IN AFRICA

MUSIC in the African tradition follows the individual throughout their lives from the cradle to the grave,(1) i.e. from the lullaby, the work and community song, to the funeral dirge. Rhythm plays an important part in daily life. The heartbeat displays rhythm, so does breathing, also walking.

Music is the highly abstract art of organising sound. It requires the high order thinking skills of the musicians to combine highly abstract concepts. It requires the high order thinking skills of the listeners to understand and appreciate highly abstract concepts. The key abstract concept is sound.

Like language, there are rules for the organisation of sounds (or music) and there are traditions of sounds (or music). Music can be understood by the listener if they understand the rules, and are part of the culture from which the music came.(2)

It is important to distinguish the value of the spoken word from music. Songs are poems set to music, but the musical understanding comes from understanding the melody (or 'tune'), the combination of sounds (or 'harmony'), the rhythms, and finally the sound qualities (or 'timbre'). It is this combination of the sound elements and NOT the meaning of the words of the poem that inspire, move, or elevate the human consciousness AS MUSIC. Poetry is a separate art form entirely and needs a separate discussion.

Most listeners, journalists, rock critics and pundits confuse music with poetry. They will typically judge a piece of music based on the poetic qualities of the song lyrics and not the aesthetic qualities of how the musicians have combined sounds. In addition, it is easier for journalists to write about song lyrics than it is for them to describe sounds in words. It is worth noting that most of them have literary and not musical backgrounds. Moreover, it is easier to get a 'hit' with good quality poetry (i.e. commercial song lyrics) than with good quality music. There are, of course, artists that have brilliantly combined music and poetry.

The first musical instrument was probably the voice.(3) The earliest compositions were probably poems set to music, which produces 'songs.'

Another early musical form was the vocable, a vocal composition of humming or 'nonsense' syllables--an early form of Scat singing.(4)

The use of hands or sticks to accompany the voice was probably the next development. Hand clapping or the hitting of sticks gave this early music a rhythmic propulsion.

The third major development was the drum, an instrument that had the advantage of being easy to make. Handclapping or drumming animated the feet through dance.(5) With the birth of dance, came a completely new artistic form but in truth, this too would require another paper just by itself.

The Black musical tradition follows African history. This history is the oldest on earth. East Africa is the birthplace of the human race. The oldest skeletons of our species were found there.(6) The evidence for the world's oldest civilisations were found in Sudan and in Egypt.(7) The once fashionable theories claiming that the Black race came from somewhere other than Africa, or that the Ancient Egyptians were non-Negroes, were publicly exploded in the 1970s.(8)

Figure 1. According to Dr Davidson, this is an image of: 'DANCING IN PROCESSION ... men wear decorative, flared leggings, and what appear to be masks. Women are shown with rounded stomachs and long, ribbon-like head-dresses.'(10) The picture credits claim this image was originally 6000 to 4000 BC.(11)

# The Black Musical Tradition

Figure 2, to cite Davidson once more, shows: 'MAKING MUSIC, one man strums a stringed instrument while another holds a long, stick-like object, possibly a kind of flute. Both musicians are wearing feathers on their heads.'(12) The picture credits claim this image was originally 800 to 700 BC.(13)

Ancient Egypt may well represent the beginnings of African music as far as we know. However, there are images of music making and processional dance from the Algerian Sahara that are very old and may challenge the idea of Egyptian beginnings (figures 1 and 2). Dr Basil Davidson, the great English Africanist, even called this Saharan evidence 'The Oldest Africans.'(9) The Rock Paintings of the Sahara are many thousands of years old and may date back as early as 8000 BC for the earliest images. By the very nature of this rock art, the images are hard to date and it is thus possible that some of the activities represented in this Algerian art predates activities in Ancient Egypt.

Ancient Egypt may well represent the second phase of African music making. The musicologist, Carl Engel, wrote a masterpiece on music in the ancient world called *The Music of the Most Ancient Nations.* According to him, Ancient Egypt was a source of musical instruments, musical theory, and a place where the performance of music reach sophisticated levels.(14)

Other wall carvings show ensembles of a harp, tamboura and a man clapping, another shows two harpists performing, yet another shows a harp accompanied by a tambourine. The harps themselves were sometimes very large indeed. One is shown with 13 strings but unfortunately we do not know what pitches the strings were tuned to. Carl Engel believes they were tuned to the pentatonic scale (i.e. a type of 5 note scale). I, however, see no

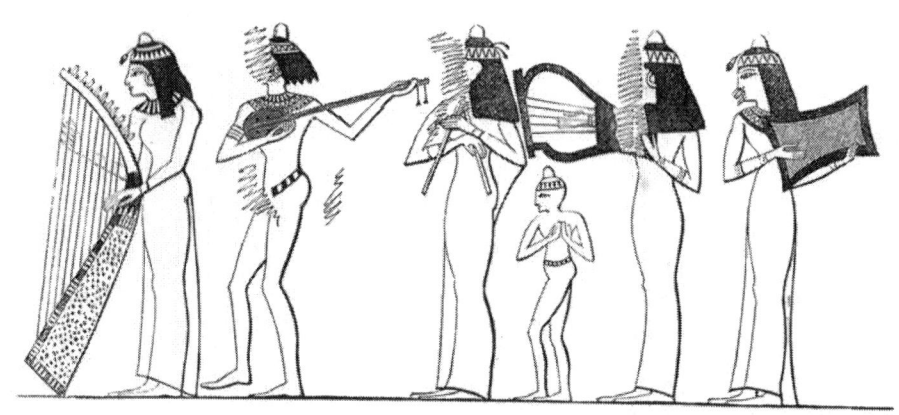

Figure 3 shows an ensemble of female musicians playing the harp, the tamboura (i.e. the lute), the double-pipe, the lyre and the tambourine. A girl is clapping along. It is very unlikely that these instruments played in unison even at the octave thus each instrument would have played its own unique part.

reason why they were not tuned to the diatonic scale (i.e. a type of 7 or 8 note scale). I give my reasons for this conjecture below (see information on Obenga).

Other wall carvings show that the Ancient Egyptians invented or developed the pipe (i.e. a wind instrument that may have possessed a reed and played a pentatonic scale), the trumpet (probably made of wood), the drum (some played by hands, others with beaters), the tambourine, the sistrum (also played in Ethiopia), the cymbals and the bells.

According to Professor Ashenafi Kebede, an Ethiopian musicologist and a leading authority on Black music, the Ancient Egyptians were the first people in the world to experiment with the idea of creating musical notation (i.e. a way of writing down music). They created the first society where it was possible to make a profession out of performing music. They had schools where it was possible to study music, both vocal performance and instrumental performance. These musical academies also taught musical theory and chironomy which is the art of musical notation using gesture.(17)

Even in the time of the ancient Greeks, musical theory was still being taught in Egypt. Many writers suggest that the harmonic theories attributed to Pythagoras were in fact the theories that the Egyptians taught him during his twenty two years of study in Egypt.(18) For instance, Hunter Adams III, an African American science writer, wrote: 'The Egyptians were the first to formalize the mathematical properties of music ... This mathematical

# The Black Musical Tradition

Figure 4. The harp.

Figure 5 shows the lyre, another stringed instrument. This instrument is still played in Nubia today (i.e. Southern portion of modern Egypt and Northern Sudan). Mohammed Gubara, a Nubian, is considered a leading performer on this instrument in our times.

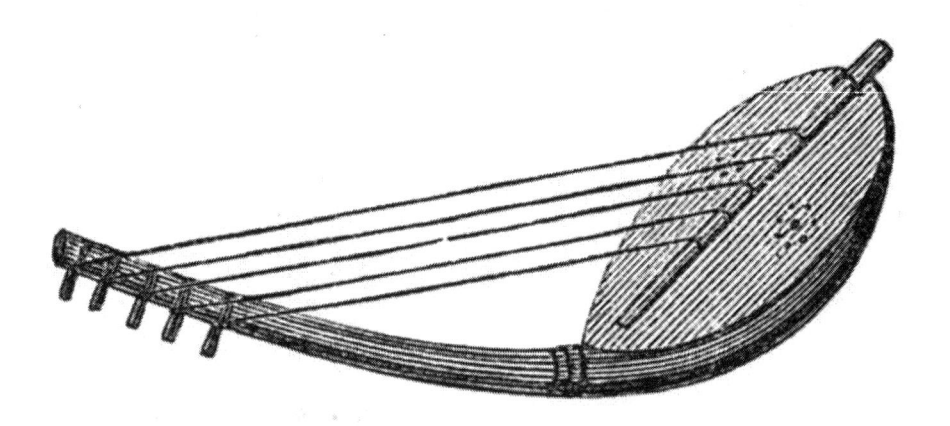

Figure 6 shows what Engel calls a 'curious instrument.'(15) Engel found this five stringed instrument curious because it 'resembles in construction the sancho, a small stringed instrument of the negroes of Guinea. It likewise bears a resemblance to the valga, found in Senegambia, Guinea, and other districts of Western Africa--an instrument which is also known by other names, as wambee, kissumba, &c.'(16)

# The Black Musical Tradition                                                13

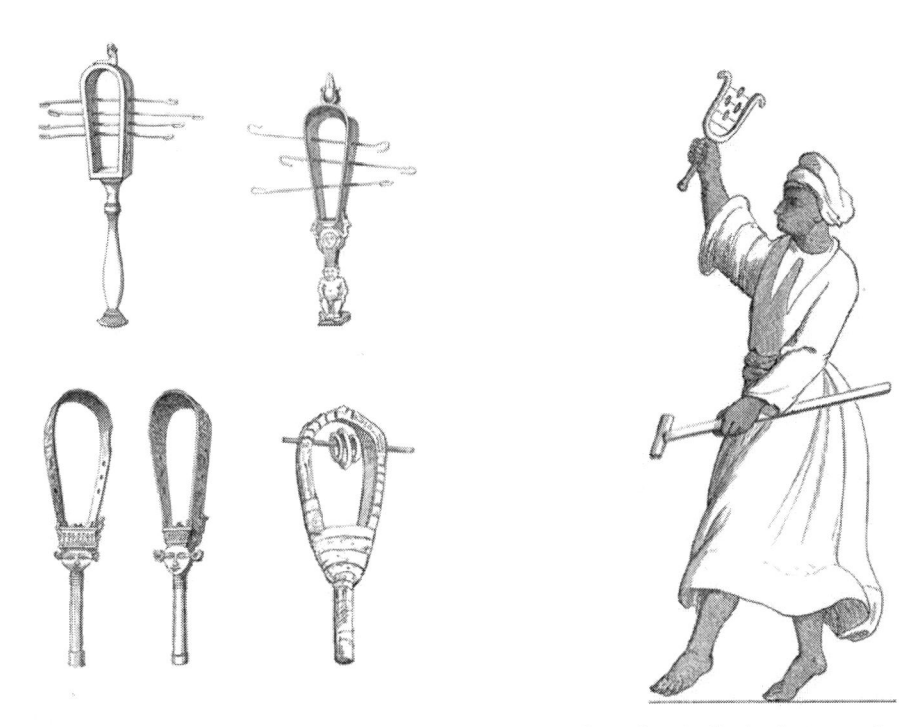

Figure 7. Taken from Engel's research, these images show the similarity between the Ancient Egyptian sistrum (left) and the Ethiopian equivalent the sansanel (right).

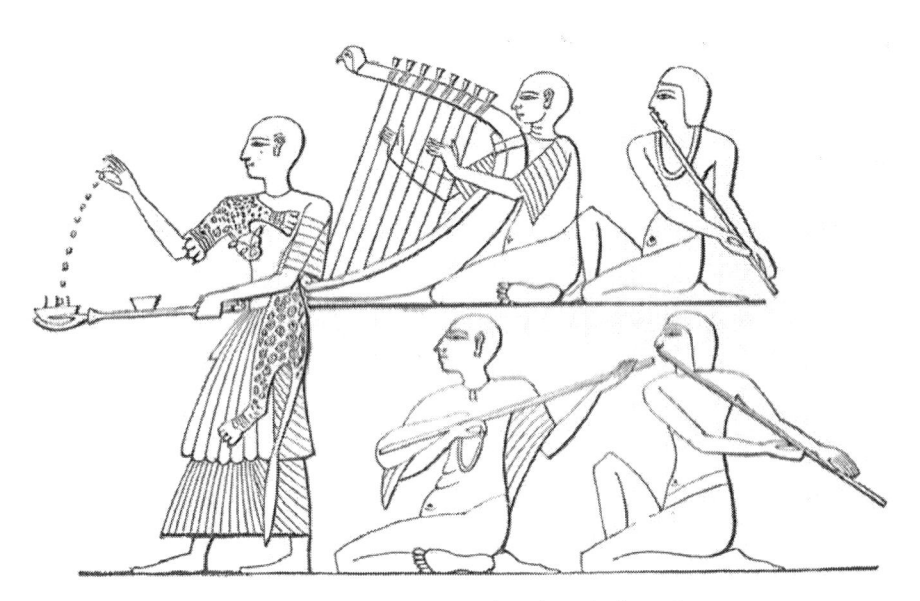

Figure 8 shows an ensemble of musicians playing liturgical music.

**Figure 9 shows a military band of trumpets and drums.**

relationship, which results from the phenomenon of classical gravitation, constitutes the essential basis of musical harmony, one of the direct applications of which is the length of a harp string. The longest string emits a sound of a certain pitch. Another string, half this one's length, emits a sound consisting of vibrations twice as rapid, and one octave higher. Thus all the intervals which define the seven notes of the diatonic scale represent the relationship between the string-lengths for any two notes which is the inverse of the relationship between their rates of vibration.'(19)

According to Professor Théophile Obenga, the great Congolese scholar, the Ancient Egyptians invented the diatonic or *do re mi fa so la te do* scale. This scale is the basis of contemporary western music. Its origins can be traced back to flutes recovered from Ancient Egyptian tombs and studied by Victor Loret, a French Egyptologist of the nineteenth century. The diatonic scale, like the Egyptian musical instruments, has diffused over Africa and the rest of the world. Thirty of these instruments have been found that play the scale. Professor Obenga is of the opinion that these flutes have been in use since at least the Fifth Dynasty period.(20)

As suggested earlier, Ancient Egyptian musical ideas may have survived amongst the music of the Nubians. Some of it has also survived in the music of the Coptic churches of Egypt and Ethiopia. Ancient Egypt was a source of many musical instruments for Africa and for the rest of the world. The harp, the lute, the reed clarinet, the talking drum, and the sistrum were played in Egypt.

# The Black Musical Tradition

Figure 10. Seventeenth century etching of musicians and a dancer from the Kingdom of Ndongo (in modern Angola).

The fall of Ancient Egypt was followed by the rise of great medieval African empires. Ancient Ghana rose in West Africa followed by Medieval Mali and the Songhai Empire. In the Nigeria region, the Empire of Benin became important. In South West Africa, the Angolan Kingdoms of Ndongo and Matamba became powerful. In Southern Africa, the powerful Munhumutapa Empire arose.(21)

The royal courts of these states patronised musicians, producing a number of Classical Music traditions. The masses had lives surrounded by music from the lullaby, to the work song, to the funeral dirge. This folk music is also called Traditional Music. Finally, the twentieth century led to people of different countries hearing each other's music through the role of the mass media, especially recordings and radio. Increasing urbanisation has also had an impact, resulting in a number of Popular Music traditions.(22)

To give some details of the Classical or Courtly forms, Ancient Ethiopia has a distinguished tradition of music. One of the oldest traditions is the Fellasha chants of the Beta Israel community. Since the Beta Israel practise one of the oldest forms of Judaism in the world, it follows that the origin of their religious music may be equally old. Their music is almost entirely vocal but during the New Year or Rosh Hashanah celebrations, the vocal music is traditionally accompanied by sistums, drums and bells. The lyrics were based on sacred biblical texts sung rubato (i.e. where the performer can bend the time) but combining syllabic and melismatic styles. Long melismas were sung with vibrato with a throbbing and nasal vocal quality. The chanted prayers were divided into ten styles based on the ten times of performance in a day--sunrise, forenoon, midday, afternoon, before sunset, sunset, bedtime, midnight, before dawn and dawn.(23)

Ethiopia, also home to one of the very oldest Christian traditions in the world, has an important tradition of Christian church music. Saint Yared (476-571), an Ethiopian saint, is believed to have invented the Ethiopian system of musical notation, but not all the evidence is in agreement with this view. Some say musical notation was invented a thousand years later. Less controversially, Saint Yared wrote a collection of hymns known as the *Deggwa* that are still sung today. Professor Kebede gives an example of a Church hymn sung accompanied by a kebero or drum and handclapping.(24) We shall have more to say on Ethiopian music, see below.

The Empire of Mali in West Africa had a very rich musical tradition. As a kingdom, Sundiata Keita founded it in 1240 AD. In the following century, it became a powerful empire. Sundiata Keita is a distant ancestor of the musician Salif Keita. Malian music has continued to exercise a huge influence over West African music. Moreover, many scholars including Dalby, see below, believe that The Blues, the pre-eminent African American musical form, is of Malian origin.

Winifred Dalby wrote learnedly about the music of the Malians.(25) She gave the example of Ibn Battuta who visited the Empire of Mali in 1352 and had much to say on the performances of music and dance that he witnessed. He described musicians playing gold and silver plated ganabir (i.e. lutes). Moreover, military musicians played drums, horns and trumpets as the emperor took his seat. Another dignitary played an instrument of reeds which Dalby identifies as the balafon (i.e. xylophone) over which he chanted a poem praising the emperor and recounting his battles and deeds of bravery.

Richard Jobson, an English visitor to the region in 1620 and 1621, described the music in some detail. According to him: 'There is, without doubt, no people on the earth more naturally affected to the sound of music that these people; which the principal [i.e. elite] persons do hold as an ornament of their state, so as when we come to see them, their music will

**Figure 11. A 1925 griot convention resulting in a kora ensemble.**

seldom be wanting, wherein they have a perfect resemblance to the Irish Rhymer sitting in the same manner as they do upon the ground, somewhat remote from the company; and as they use singing of Songs unto their music, the ground and effect whereof is the rehearsal of the ancient stock of the King, exalting his ancestry, and recounting over all the worthy and famous acts by him or them has been achieved: singing likewise *extempore* upon any occasion is offered, whereby the principal may be pleased.'(26)

This is a description of the art of the griots. Jobson is here describing praise singing. Some of the performances are *extempore* or improvised. This is the difficult art of composing and performing on the spot, real time. Jazz is based on the same concept.

In the next excerpt, Jobson describes the main musical instrument, the balafon, i.e. xylophone: '[F]irst I would acquaint you of their most principal instrument, which is called Ballards [i.e. balafon] made to stand a foot above the ground, hollow under, and has upon the top some seventeen wooden keys standing like the Organ, upon which he that plays sitting upon the ground, just against the middle of the instrument, strikes with a stick in either hand, about a foot long, at the end whereof is made fast a round ball, covering with some soft stuff, to avoid the clattering noise the bare sticks would make.'(27)

In the following excerpt, he describes two musical instruments. One of them matches the description given by musicologist Carl Engel of the sancho (also called the valga, wambee, kissumba, etc.), see figure 6 above. This was a stringed instrument sharing some vague affinities to a lute or harp. The sancho evolved into the kora. The second instrument is the

Figure 12 showing a gonje. According to Salem Ould Elhadj, a Timbuktu historian, cultured and aristocratic women played the fiddle in Timbuktu in a domestic context amongst other women and for their husbands. After dinner, the wife would burn incense as a seductive prelude followed by serenading her husband. She typically improvised lyrics that exalted her husband's ancestors and thanked him for the things he brought to her that contributed to her material, spiritual and moral development. It was also the custom to ask the man's forgiveness for things that she may have done. Traditionally, she played until her husband slept.

talking drum: '[T]hat which is the most common in use, is made of a great gourd, and a neck thereunto fastened ... but they have no manner of fret, and the strings they are either such as the place yields, or their invention can attain to make, being very unapt to yield a sweet and musical sound, notwithstanding with pins they wind and bring to agree in tuneable notes, having not above six strings upon their greatest instrument: In consortship with this they have many times another who plays upon a little drum which he holds under his left arm, and with a crooked stick in his right hand, and his naked fingers on the left he strikes the drum.'(28)

Kora music is still popular today in West Africa. Kora music, like much of Africa's music is harmonically static. It is structured on one simple bass line that repeats itself. The music has a strong dance beat orientation. The use of back-beat compels even the unwilling listener to respond to the music by patting their feet, clicking their fingers or nodding their heads.

# The Black Musical Tradition

Kora performances often involve two musicians, one to play the accompaniment, the other, the melody lines. The accompanist's job is to lay down the bass line, chords and the groove, while the other player spontaneously improvises. The musicians are renowned for an astonishing and brilliant level of virtuosic interplay. Famous kora masters include the Konte family of the Gambia, and the Nigerian virtuoso, Tunde Jegede, who has popularised the music in the UK.

Jobson also mentions fiddlers playing music, which, incidentally, shows that Africa also had bowed instruments. Professor Nketia, an expert on African music, says that the one-string fiddle has a wide distribution over the savannah belt of West Africa where they called it a goge, goje or a gonje. The string and bow was made of horsehair.(29)

In the West African Empire of Songhai, the kings and emperors each had royal ensembles of trumpets and drums that marched ahead of them when they were in public. The armed forces had ensembles of trumpets and drums. They also had griots, i.e. troubadours or praise singers. The imperial court had vocal music consisting of a solo singer accompanied by a choir. Mahmud Kati, one of the Timbuktu chroniclers, mentions agricultural slaves gathering to the sound of drums and flutes. They worked to the sound of the drums. He also mentioned ensembles of flautists playing at the royal court. He specifies 40 flautists in one passage.(30)

In the Empire of Munhumutapa, the main instrument was the mbira (or thumb piano). Played at the royal courts, the instrument had a wide distribution across Zimbabwe, Zambia and Mozambique. The mbira player either plays solo, producing very beautiful and tranquil music, or plays to accompany the voice. Typical compositions will include story-songs, epics and ballads. Performers may alternate musical episodes and sung passages. Performers may laugh, sing, talk, whistle or yodel during the performances. Some compositions have refrains for the audience to join in with.(31)

In Northern Africa and the Middle East the Oriental Tradition developed. The musical forms of Ancient Egypt, Ancient Ethiopia (i.e. Axum), and North Africa had much in common with each other. The Arab invasion and conquest of Northern Africa led to Islamic texts being used as song material, adding a poetic dimension, but not necessarily changing the musical forms.(32) The Islamic contribution was founded by Bilal, an Ethiopian by origin, and one of the founders of Islam. His composition, *The Azan* (The Call to Prayer), was Islam's first musical composition.(33)

The Arabs and their African converts invaded and occupied Spain from 710 until 1492 AD, spreading the Oriental style there and changing Spanish music for ever. Spanish music is so obviously African influenced that other European nations use this as an excuse to look down on Spanish music. The Cairo Musical Academy was a distinguished centre of musical training in the Middle Ages. In 822 Ziryab, a Black Middle Eastern gentleman and style guru, founded the Cordovan Musical Academy in Spain. He was the leading lutenist and singer of the period as well as being one of the most refined men of any era.(34)

The lute was an important instrument in this tradition. Of Ancient Egyptian origins, it spread across North Africa and even to Europe, via Spain, where it was the most important courtly instrument of the sixteenth century.(35) The voice was also important. A highly developed singing style was cultivated with a powerful vibrato and much ornamentation.(36) The spread of musical and cultural ideas from Africa to Spain, and from Spain to the rest of Europe, demonstrates the African roots of certain aspects of European classical music.

In the rest of Africa, in the urban centres, a series of Polyrhythmic Dance styles emerged.(37) Polyrhythm, i.e. many rhythms happening at once, is easily demonstrated by a drum choir. One drummer plays one rhythm, while another drummer plays something different, yet a third drummer plays something different. The result is a series of interlocking patterns out of which a groove emerges. The polyrhythmic impetus can come from any combination of voices or instruments playing different patterns simultaneously.(38) Music from various parts of Africa, ranging from Highlife (West Africa) to Mbaqanga (South Africa), are remarkably similar in the way polyrhythms are used.

## CHAPTER 2: EVOLUTION IN THE DIASPORA

AFRICAN AMERICAN music is based on the African background in many ways. It is easy to show the African imprint on certain African American songs, dances, instruments and processions. African American musicians, however, freely borrowed and adapted musical ideas from other peoples, including Europeans and European Americans. Finally, African Americans constructed brand new musical forms that are wholly American even if some of the building blocks came from Africa, the Caribbean or Europe.

The instruments that were carried over to the Americas by enslaved Africans included the banjo, the xylophone, gongs, rattles, castanets, the thumb piano, flutes, clarinets, wooden and ivory trumpets, bagpipes and drums.(39)

However, European enslavers were not happy about African culture being brought to the Americas. They enforced restrictive enslavement laws called the 'Black Codes.' In the US, this legislation led to the legal suppression of the drum. The drum was considered dangerous to the enslavers since many African states had drum scripts.(40) With tonal languages, the meaning of a spoken word was determined by the sound of the word and the pitch at which it was said. The talking drum could copy the sounds of the rising and falling of pitches and was thus used to communicate with large numbers of people.(41)

This legislation had a dramatic and negative impact on African American music! The suppression of the drum changed African American music from being polyrhythmic (i.e. many rhythms being played at the same time) to becoming monorhythmic (i.e. one rhythm being played at a time). This is why the African American musical tradition developed differently to other African-derived musics of the western hemisphere. The polyrhythmic complexity of the Ancestors was suppressed.(42)

The oldest African American music was the Call and the Cries. Enslaved Africans on plantations would convert spoken messages into songs that would be sung to pass on information to others on the plantation. The Calls had lyrics that summoned plantation workers to eat, broke the monotony of work or warned the inattentive plantation worker about the coming of a white overseer. The Cries were more emotionally intense and had lyrics that covered loneliness, lovesickness or hunger. Singers employed African vocal techniques such as melismas, tonal glides, falsetto and yodels. The Calls and Cries evolved into three main musical genres--the Spirituals, the Work Songs, and the Dance Songs.(43)

The Spirituals are a unique artistic tradition.(44) No other people had spirituals and there are no European equivalents to them. The compositions themselves often had a social context with clear messages of freedom for the enslaved. For example: "Go down Moses and tell ol' Pharaoh, let my people go". In addition to social commentary, the music had a religious function.(45) Sung in and out of church at births, baptisms, festivals, etcetera, the Spirituals were sung with call and response using vocal shouts, moans and slides accompanied by dance or handclapping.(46)

The Work Songs had their origins in West and South Africa, though the tradition is older than this. Work songs were sung in Ancient Egypt.(47) Sung during field, railroad, lumberjacking, fishing or chain gang work, the main feature was the repeated crash or heavy beat on the first (or last) beat of each phrase coinciding with the swinging of pickaxes or other rhythmical work activity. A lead singer would set the pace for the singing and the work for the group.(48)

Another branch of Work Songs were the Sea Shanties. Wikipedia says: 'In the first few decades of the 19th century, White European-American culture, especially the Anglophone--the sailors' "Cheer'ly Man" and some capstan songs notwithstanding--was not known for its work songs. By contrast, African workers, both in Africa and in the New World, were widely noted to sing while working. The fact that Euro-American observers found African work-singers so remarkable (as can be gleaned from the tone of their descriptions) suggests that work songs were indeed rather foreign to their culture. Such references begin to appear in the late 18th century, whence one can see the cliché develop that Black Africans "could not" work without singing. For example, an observer in Martinique in 1806 wrote, "The negroes have a different air and words for every kind of labour; sometimes they sing, and their motions, even while cultivating the ground, keep time to the music." So while the depth of the African-American work song traditions is now recognized, in the early 19th century they stood in stark contrast to the paucity of such traditions among Euro-Americans. Thus while European sailors had learned to put short chants to use for certain kinds of labor, the paradigm of a comprehensive system of

## The Black Musical Tradition

developed work songs for most tasks may have been contributed by the direct involvement of or through the imitation of African-Americans.'(49)

Finally the Dance Song, usually accompanied by the fiddle, was music to move the feet.(50)

African American music contains a number of distinct musical elements. The dance beat orientation compels and charms the unwilling listener to move to the music.(51) The 'blue notes' are tones altered from the *do re mi fa so la te do* scale. They are lowered versions of the third note *mi* and the seventh note *te*, giving the music a distinctive African tonal quality.(52) The call and response, a technique where a lead singer sings a line and the choir respond in a question and answer fashion, is an exceedingly ancient idea used in Ancient Egypt and elsewhere in Africa.(53) Early European classical music is also dominated by this technique.(54) It even dominates Black group dynamics outside music. At political or religious meetings where someone addresses the crowd, they can expect the response of "Amen!" or "Word!" A final feature of this tradition is the emotionally elevating context where the musicians work to elevate the consciousness of the listener by the use of blue notes, call and response, etcetera. Some of these techniques are also used by preachers in the church.

By the late nineteenth century, Black American music consisted of four types of music--Gospel, Blues, Brass band and Ragtime.(55)

Gospel was a development from the Spirituals. It represented the increasing political, economic, and social role of the Black church. Richard Allen the founding bishop of the African Methodist Episcopal Church was a key link in the evolution of Black sacred music from Spirituals towards Gospel. He published a hymnal for his congregation in 1801 entitled, *A Collection of Spiritual Songs and Hymns Selected from Various Authors by Richard Allen, African Minister.* Consisting of 54 hymns, Allen selected material popular with the White Methodists. This exposed Black congregations directly to non-African musical material. Consequently, when Jubilee Music (later called Gospel) emerged a couple of generations later, the music had already absorbed a greater use of non-African melodies and harmonies. There is also a theory that some of gospel's non-African influences came from the vocal music of Scotland. In time, however, all these elements were African Americanised. The Fisk University Jubilee Singers were important in taking Gospel around the world, performing in Germany, Switzerland and Britain. By the 1920s Thomas Dorsey, composer of *Precious Lord, Take My Hand,* would emerge as the most important composer of the genre.(56)

**Figure 13.** The Fisk University Jubilee Singers.

Blues developed from the Work song. However, it was and is the most misunderstood of all of Black America's music. The Blues has nothing to do with whinging in self-pity. On the contrary, it is happy music representing the triumph of the soul over adversity. The adversity is the blues but the music is the antidote to that adversity.(57) Using the three primary chords of European music, many blues compositions followed a set musical pattern where each verse is twelve bars or measures in length. This musical structure ultimately influenced Jazz, Soul and popular music for the next hundred years.(58) Ma Rainey was the first professional blues singer who elevated the art, and she was a great influence on Bessie Smith, the 'Empress of the Blues'. William Christopher Handy, often called the 'Father of the Blues', was the first to collect and publish blues songs (in 1912).(59) His songbooks went on to influence Black music for the next two generations.

Brass Bands were an outgrowth of the military band. Black military bands had been in existence since 1812 (60) but the invention of new brass instruments in the 1840s by the Belgian Adolphe Sax made these instruments available. These instruments were largely ignored in Europe (except by the British working class), however the Creoles of New Orleans

# The Black Musical Tradition

Figure 14. Louis Armstrong the great Jazzman recorded W. C. Handy's songs in 1955. The recordings were played to an old and blind Handy who was moved to tears by Armstrong's jazz interpretations.

started a tradition of their own. They used brass instruments to accompany their processions, such as the Mardi Gras festival, which involved a troupe of dancers and musicians parading down New Orleans streets (61) often twirling umbrellas. The festival, clearly of African origin, can be compared to the yearly procession of King of Benin (in the ancient Nigeria region), a tradition going back hundreds of years.(62) The use of the umbrellas in processions was popular with the Ashantis of Ghana as can be seen in a celebrated 1819 sketch of the Yam Festival.(63) Another important feature of Brass band music was the rebirth of the drum, as it was the only African American music to use the instrument at that time.

Figure 15. Bessie Smith, 'the Empress of the Blues'.

# The Black Musical Tradition

**Figure 16. Scott Joplin, the King of Ragtime.**

Finally, Ragtime was a music associated with the piano. Scott Joplin, composer of *The Entertainer* was king of the idiom. Ragtime was based on the dance beat emphasised by the pianist's left hand. The left hand would play a bass note followed by chord, followed by another bass note, followed by a chord, giving a *boof cha boof cha*. This was called 'striding.' The right hand would play the melody based on complicated rhythms with banjo-like, hence African-derived, phrases. This was called 'ragging.'(64) The musical layout and structure of each ragtime composition was, however, patterned exactly on European American military and brass band marches. Clearly, this musical synthesis was for virtuoso performers. Among the masters of Ragtime were James Scott and Eubie Blake.

Jazz synthesised elements from the Blues, Brass band and Ragtime.(65) From the Blues, jazzmen took the twelve bar structure, the call and response, and the blue notes. From the Brass bands, they took the drums, and from Ragtime, they took the dance beat and the virtuosity. Buddy Bolden, the great brass player at the turn of the century 'whose dance-beat orientation went all the way back to the last days of the ancestral dances in Congo Square'(66) was the first to synthesise these elements. Moreover he created the first jazz groove called the Big Four. Bringing instrumental improvisation into the mix, he gave the first jazz performance in August

**Figure 17. The Louis Armstrong Hot Five.**

1894 when his musicians improvised "a hot blues." A distinguished jazzman, Jelly Roll Morton, remembered him as the Pied Piper of the New Orleans dancers: "We'd heard old Buddy's trumpet and we'd all start ... He'd turn his trumpet around toward the city and blow his blues, calling his children home, as he used to say."(67)

1925 saw the rise of Louis Armstrong, distinguished as the greatest trumpeter in history, greatest of the jazzmen, and its first superstar. His Hot Five and Hot Seven ensembles set the tone and the musical standards for the New Orleans and Chicago schools.(68) His Hot Seven had a frontline of trumpet, clarinet and trombone, and a rhythm section of piano, banjo, tuba and drums. While this music had none of the polyrhythmic complexity of African or Black South American music, the fact that four musicians were entrusted to carry the rhythm was highly significant. His performances alternated group improvisation for the three frontline horns (trumpet, trombone and clarinet) accompanied by the rhythm section and sung or solo improvised passages accompanied by the rhythm section.

# The Black Musical Tradition

When the three horns improvised it sometimes evoked the spiritual power of gospel music. On the other hand, the solo improvisations allowed Louis Armstrong to display his singular technical and artistic brilliance.

Mr Armstrong was also a great pacesetter for many aspects of Black style, even today.(69) His greeting of "What you say?" has become "Weh yu a seh?" in the Caribbean and elsewhere. The mumbo-jumbo handshaking routine is still as hip as ever. Nor should we forget his huge influence on Black men's fashion.(70) The other great jazzmen from the early days were King Oliver and Sidney Bechet.

Swing began in New York in the early thirties with the Fletcher Henderson Orchestra. The swing ensemble grew to a 'big band' typically with four saxophonists who also doubled on clarinets, four trumpeters and four trombonists. Propelling the new music was a rhythm section of piano, guitar, double bass and drums. The bass player 'walked', playing one note per beat, while the drummer 'rode' playing a distinctive 6 against the bass player's 4 rhythm on the ride cymbal.(71) Kansas City birthed a revolutionary and highly improvised form of Swing led by Count Basie. His rhythm section was the hardest swinging and most influential of all. He led an orchestra, whose music was blues and call & response based, with such a lightening effect that it sounded as if the Holy Ghost had struck.(72) The great artists of the Swing era included Ella Fitzgerald 'the First Lady of Swing', the Chick Webb Orchestra, and the Jimmie Lunceford Orchestra. Lester Young, a great tenor saxophonist, was a particularly brilliant improviser from the period. Duke Ellington, whose career far outlasted the Swing era, ultimately became the best, the most innovative and the most important composer in American history.

In Cuba, a different tradition was developing, associated with Mario Bauza, one time musical director of the Chick Webb Orchestra, and his family relative Franz Machito. The laxer enforcement of the Black Codes in Cuba meant that the drum was not suppressed by law. Cuban musicians therefore retained the polyrhythmic complexity of the Ancestors.(73) As with African music Afro-Cuban music was harmonically static and was based on a variety of African-derived modal scales. Bauza and Machito mixed the Cuban polyrhythmic music with the orchestral jazz and high level instrumental improvisation of Henderson and Basie. Machito's rhythm section, however, consisted of four drummers as well as a piano and bass.

The popular dances were the Mambo, the Cha Cha Cha and the Rhumba. Meanwhile the Brazilian and Colombian musicians were producing related

30                                          The Black Musical Tradition

Figure 18. Franz Machito (centre).

Figure 19. Dizzy Gillespie, founder of the Modern Jazz scene.

# The Black Musical Tradition

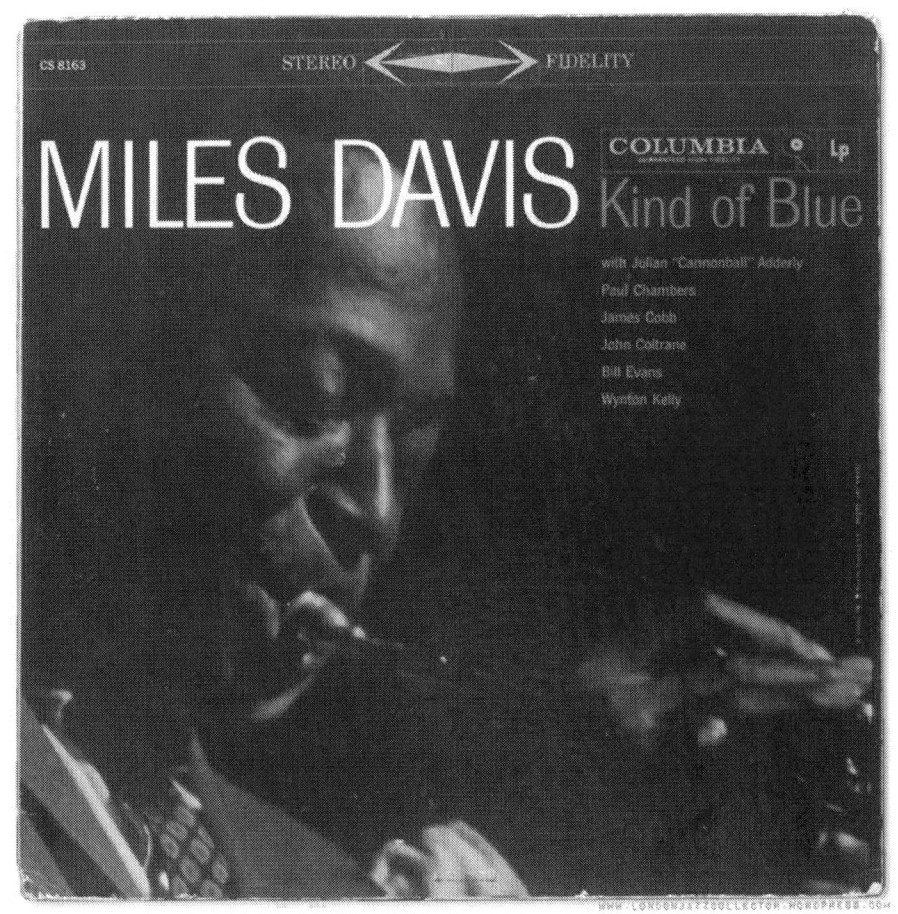

**Figure 20. Miles Davis'** *Kind of Blue,* **1959, is widely regarded as the finest modern jazz album ever recorded.**

musical forms. Celia Cruz was the Queen of the Cuban musicians. The music of this region, including Calypso and Zouk, show stylistic commonalties to the polyrhythmic dance music mentioned above.(74)

Another revolution took place in the Jazz world in 1944.(75) Trumpeter Dizzy Gillespie, alto saxophonist Charlie Parker and pianist Thelonius Monk created Modern Jazz in a now legendary series of jam sessions at the Henry Minton's Playhouse in Harlem. This was music for the concert stage and nightclub, but not the dance hall. Accompanied by a rhythm section of just a piano, double bass and drums, modern jazz was technically brilliant, representing the very highest levels of musicianship ever reached. Their performances involved long, daring extended improvisations, played at breakneck speed, accompanied by a barrage of drum talk. The drummer engaged in a musical discussion with the other instruments in the band, making a lyrical instrument of the drum for the first time in African American music. Unfortunately, hostile media criticism resulted in Modern Jazz being shrouded in controversy.(76) The music attracted a young Black male following, like Hip Hop does today, but was fast losing its mass Black appeal.

As an underground movement, Modern Jazz evolved into Cool Jazz in 1948, Hard Bop in 1955, the Avant-Garde by 1960, and Soul Jazz by 1961. Miles Davis was by far the most important musician of the modernist era recording far more classics and masterpieces than anyone else. Other important luminaries included the Modern Jazz Quartet, Art Blakey and the Jazz Messengers, the John Coltrane Quartet, the Ornette Coleman Quartet and the Jimmy Smith Trio. Though no longer popular with big audiences, the high quality of the music produced by these artists won great international respect for the artistry and intellect of the African Americans.

## CHAPTER 3: FROM SOUL TO GRIME

THE 1950s saw the rise of three challenges to Modern Jazz--Rock and Roll, Rockabilly and Secularised Gospel Music.

Rock and Roll was an aggressive simplified development of the Blues for an urban market. Concentrating on simple sung verses with little instrumental improvisation, a key feature of this music was its ability to cross over into the mainstream i.e. White market. Its founders were Fats Domino, Little Richard, Bo Diddley and Ike Turner. Fats Domino was the first to cross over and sell a million records. Little Richard combined a gospel vocal style with a ferocious energy. Bo Diddley invented rock guitar playing by incorporating drum-based rhythms into the guitarist's repertoire. Ike Turner's *Rocket 88* recorded in 1951 is regarded as the first real Rock and Roll recording.(77)

Rockabilly was a synthesis of Rock and Roll with a white folk idiom called Hillbilly music. Most of its musical elements came from the Blues, but its lyrical and storytelling elements came from white folk forms. Ironically, the founder of this synthesis was none other than Chuck Berry. His influence has dominated popular music to this very day. His lyrics spoke to the concerns and aspirations of young White America.(78)

Ray Charles, first of the Soul musicians, took songs and chord changes from the Black American church and gave them secular words. His own piano style echoed that of a church pianist. His singing style had the power and grittiness of a church singer.(79) The gospel roots of his 1954 recording *I've Got a Woman* and subsequent hits are obvious. Again, the fundamentals of call and response, blues, backbeat, and a heavy emotionalism predominate. Beginning as a gospel artist, Sam Cooke evolved an urbane polished romantic soulful image. Stax and Atlantic labels continued the earthy and vibrant sound of Ray Charles into Southern Soul recording the likes of Wilson Pickett, Otis Redding, Arthur Conley, and Sam & Dave. Motown label continued the urbane polished sound of Sam Cooke to create massive crossover success with the likes of the Supremes, Temptations, Smokey Robinson and the Miracles, and Martha Reeves and the Vandellas. By 1962, a King and a Queen of Soul had been

**Figure 21. Ray Charles, the founder of Soul Music.**

crowned in the persons of James Brown and Aretha Franklin. The rise of Soul later coincided with the Black Renaissance of afros, dashikis, 'Black is beautiful,' etcetera. Even the Afro comb, which is incidentally of Ancient Egyptian origin,(80) became known as the Soul comb.

The Soul and Blues musicians had a big influence on the Caribbean island of Jamaica replacing the dominance of Lord Kitchener Calypso from Trinidad. Ska, Jamaica's first indigenous popular music was derived from African American influences.(81) The Isley Brothers original *Twist and Shout* sounds almost like something from the Blue Beat record label. The only significant difference between Ska and its American parents are the heavy and persistent off-beat accompaniment. Prince Buster was a major name in the music's development and documentation. He also recorded the drum-based music of the Rastafarian community, including their classic *Oh Carolina!* Other Ska pioneers included Laurel Aitken, Alton Ellis and Stranger Cole.

Ska soon evolved into Rocksteady and by 1968, it had evolved into Reggae. This music was typically of a leisurely speed and dominated by a *phat* bass line and two heavy off-beat chords per bar, against Ska's four. There was also the typical 'one drop' on the bass drum on the third beat of each bar. Toots and the Maytals made the first recording in this idiom called

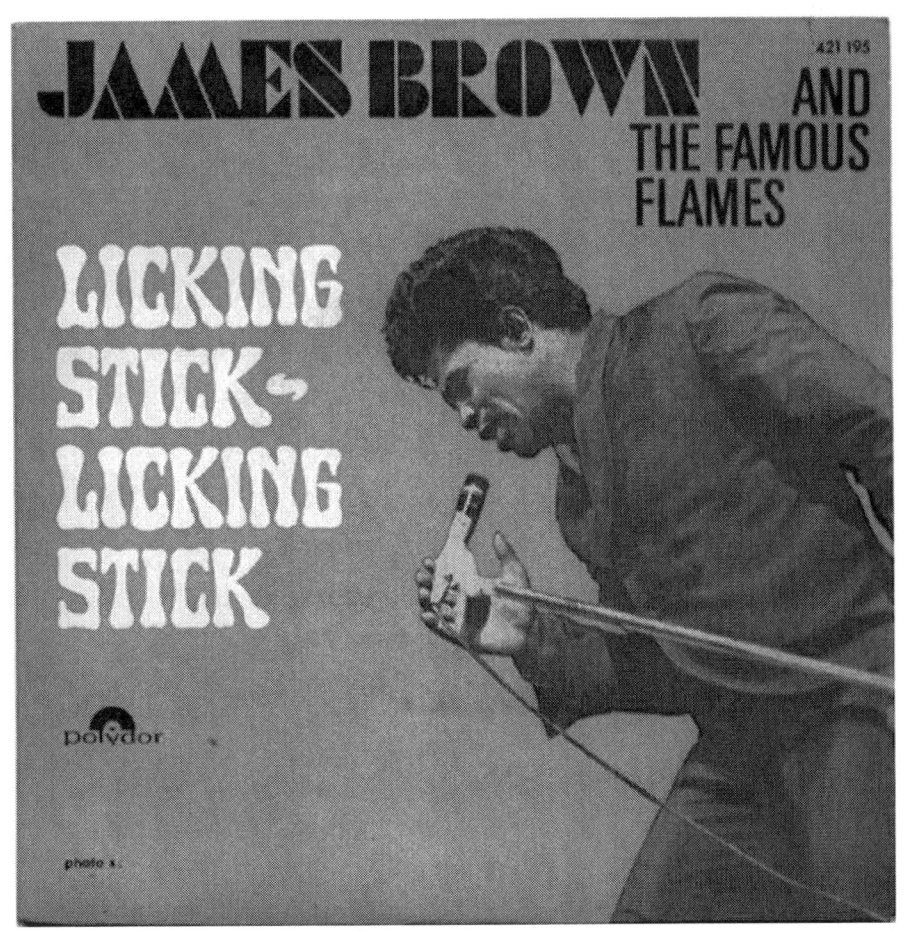

Figure 22. *Licking Stick* was one of the early James Brown Funk classics alongside *Cold Sweat* and *Say it Loud!* Funk was to directly influence Disco and Hip Hop.

*Do the Reggay* (sic) that year.(82) Jimmy Cliff was an important name in the development of Reggae as was the producer Lee 'Scratch' Perry. In time, the lyrics of reggae songs became associated with Black pride and political protest coming from the Rastafari community. This music would ultimately put Jamaica on the musical map of the world.

Meanwhile, James Brown, Soul Brother No. 1, had evolved a new style of Soul, known as Funk. This music influenced Sly Stone, Earth Wind and Fire, Kool and the Gang, and George 'Dr Funkenstein' Clinton. Funk simplified the harmonic changes that typified Soul, producing songs that were based entirely or almost entirely on one chord. In its place was a much greater rhythmic sophistication, based on polyrhythm. The bass guitarist anchored the groove by emphasising the first of every four beats, as was done with Work song. The drums, guitar, and horns played rhythmic patterns against the bass player. Out of this would emerge the typical butt-shaking funk groove.(83) Good examples of this style were James Brown's *Licking Stick* and *Say It Loud!* However, the latter recording has another distinction. Brown did not 'sing' on the recording at all, he spoke in a rhythmical fashion. The call and response between the lead and the choir was entirely spoken making this the first Rap recording (in 1968).(84)

This would appear to have influenced Jamaican music once more. In the following year, 1969, U-Roy and Big Youth, two DJ's, popularised a new style called Toasting--rhythmical talking over Reggae. The DJ art of uttering sounds over music to spur on the dancers predates this period. However, complete songs in this style did not appear until the late sixties. The 1970s saw Reggae become international through the efforts of Bob Marley. His *Natty Dread* album of 1975 brought him and Reggae music to international attention.(85)

Back in the US, two producers, Kenneth Gamble and Leon Huff, sweetened the Funk sound. They wrote catchy, sing-along melodies with the lush accompaniment of a full orchestra. Using rich compound chords and attractive counter melodies played by the violins soaring above the human voice, they gave the city of Philadelphia its own distinctive musical sound called the 'Philly Sound'.(86) Gamble and Huff produced Harold Melvin and the Blue Notes, the O Jays, and the Three Degrees. Their music, known as Disco, created a dance craze that has dominated popular music ever since. In time, Donna Summer became the Queen of Disco, with more hits than any other artist. *Her Love to Love You Baby* of 1976 was major hit and brought an overt sexuality into the music. Other important musicians in the genre were Melba Moore and Barry White.

# The Black Musical Tradition

**Figure 23. Leon Huff and Kenny Gamble, the pioneers of the Philadelphia sound. Their sound is the basis of Disco.**

In the Bronx of the early 1970s a new musical revolution was stirring. DJ Kool Herc brought the DJ culture from Jamaica to New York where he held block parties. Using two turntables, he demonstrated that it was possible to mix records together which ultimately dispensed with traditional musicianship, singers, composers, arrangers, and orchestras. This new music, called Hip Hop, required new musical skills--the ability to use two turntables, drum machines, samplers, etcetera. The DJ became the musician and the composer who could produce songs that did not need verses, choruses, or bridges. A new musical vocabulary emerged to describe the techniques that the DJs used--Backspinning, Scratching, Cutting, Mixing and Blending.

Under Afrika Bambaataa, Hip Hop evolved into a culture that combined deejaying with rapping, breaking (i.e. break dancing), tagging (i.e. graffiti art) and knowledge (i.e. the teachings of Clarence 13X, a one-time member of the Nation of Islam). His 1982 hit *Planet Rock* combined Funk and Rap with electronics and sampling.

Completing the 'Holy Trinity of Hip Hop' was Grandmaster Flash. He developed the sampling concept, showing how a DJ could sample musical passages from all of the recorded history of music.

By 1983, Run DMC became the first superstars of Hip Hop with their hit *Its Like That*. Following in their footsteps were LL Cool J who became the most important rapper in the history of the game. Public Enemy brought a strong political message over musical samples that were so thoroughly mixed, they did not even sound like recognisable samples. NWA brought the nihilism and anger of the Los Angeles street gang life to tell new and shocking stories never put on record before.(87) Since the time of these pioneers, however, Hip Hop has become less and less about the musical innovation of the DJs and more and more about the lyrical and poetic qualities of the rapper.

In the mid 1980s, Derrick May, and his school colleagues Juan Atkins and Kevin Saunderson, pioneered a completely electronic music giving the city of Detroit a new home grown sound. This style of music, known as Techno, employed computers and drum machines to produce repetitive dance rhythms. Ultimately, this resulted in lengthy soundscapes replacing the typical three-minute song making this genre unsuitable to compete in the record, CD and download charts. Instead, Techno was primarily destined for the underground club scene. Their DJs shared similar musical techniques to those pioneered by Hip Hop DJs but they created a different musical genre out of it.

In the city of Chicago, DJ Frankie Knuckles, sweetened the computer-generated sound to produce a more melodic club sound known as House. His mix of the song *I Need Your Love* is regarded as the Year 0 of House music. The other pioneers included Farley 'Jackmaster' Funk whose *Love Can't Turn Around* became a hit in the UK. Steve 'Silk' Hurley had a hit with *Jack Your Body* and Marshall Jefferson is best known for the anthem

# The Black Musical Tradition

**Figure 24. Kevin Sauderson, Derrick May, Juan Atkins, the pioneers of Techno.**

*Move Your Body.* Other pioneers, Spanky & DJ Pierre, created an experimental Chicago sound called Acid House. The new music from the Detroit and Chicago clubs eventually came to dominate the European dance scene.(88)

Bringing the story up to date: In Trinidad, there has been a fusion of Soul and Calypso, to produce Soca. In the US, there has been a fusion of Hip Hop and Soul, to produce Hip Hop Soul. In this country, there was a scene of Soul and Reggae fusion, better known as Lover's Rock. There was also a fusion of Dancehall Reggae and Rave music. This produced Jungle, which is now called Drum and Bass. There was also fusion of Jungle and US Garage, which led to UK Garage. This music is now marketed as Grime.

The technological revolution has opened the world of music to informally trained artists. Much of today's Black music is a direct result of this revolution and as long as this does not kill off the drum, much of it will stand the test of time. Unfortunately, some of the more commercial musicians of our times are losing contact with their true function as artists in the Black cultural tradition. Some produce music that celebrates a crass ghetto lifestyle, which fails to elevate, challenge, or inspire. Wynton Marsalis, among the brightest musical minds of our times, warns us against this:

"Black Codes mean a lot of things. Anything that reduces potential, that pushes your taste down to an obvious, animal level. Anything that makes you think that less significance is more enjoyable. Anything that keeps you on the surface. The way they depict women in rock videos--Black Codes. People gobbling up junk food when they can afford something better--Black Codes ... People who equate ignorance with soulfulness definitely Black Codes. The overall quality of every true artist's work is a rebellion against Black Codes. That's the line I want to be in."(89)

So should we all.

## NOTES AND REFERENCES

## Chapter 1

1. Ashenafi Kebede, *Roots of Black Music,* US, Africa World Press, 1995, pp.37-40
2. Ibidem, p.3
3. Carl Engel, *The Music of the Most Ancient Nations,* UK, John Murray, 1864, pp.9-10
4. Ashenafi Kebede, *Roots of Black Music,* p.10
5. Carl Engel, *The Music of the Most Ancient Nations,* p.10
6. Charles Finch, *Echoes of the Old Darkland,* US, Khenti, 1991, pp.1-15
7. John G. Jackson, *Ages of Gold and Silver,* US, A. A. Press, 1990, pp.70-74
8. Ivan Van Sertima ed, *Egypt Revisited,* US, Transaction Publishers, 1989, pp.9-37
9. Basil Davidson, *African Kingdoms,* Netherlands, Time-Life Books, 1966, pp.43-57
10. Ibidem, p.50
11. Ibidem, p.187
12. Ibidem, p.50
13. Ibidem, p.187
14. Carl Engel, *The Music of the Most Ancient Nations,* pp.180-276
15. Ibidem, p.211
16. Ibidem
17. Ashenafi Kebede, *Roots of Black Music,* pp.10-11
18. Théophile Obenga, *Ancient Egypt and Black Africa,* UK, Karnak House, 1992, pp.93-105
19. Hunter Havelin Adams III, *African & African-American Contributions to Science and Technology,* US, Portland Baseline Essay, 1986, p.39
20. Théophile Obenga, *Ancient Egypt and Black Africa,* pp.102-103 and George G. M. James, *Stolen Legacy,* US, U. B. C. S., 1954, p.135
21. John G. Jackson, *Introduction to African Civilisations,* US, Citadel Press, 1970 or Robin Walker, *When We Ruled,* UK, Reklaw Education, 2013
22. Adapted from Ashenafi Kebede, *Roots of Black Music,* pp.12-13
23. Ibidem, pp.22-25
24. Ibidem, pp.25-34
25. Winifred Dalby, *Music,* in *Manding Art and Civilisation,* edited by Guy Atkins, UK, Studio International 1972, pp.42-43

26. Richard Jobson, *The Golden Trade,* UK, Penguin reprint of the 1632 original, 1932, pp.143-4. In citing Jobson, I have modernised his seventeenth century spellings.
27. Ibidem, p.145
28. Ibidem, pp.144-145
29. J. H. Kwabena Nketia, *The Music of Africa,* UK, Victor Gollancz, 1974, pp.102-103
30. Robin Walker et al, *Everyday Life in an Early West African Empire,* UK, SIVEN, 2013, p.127
31. Ashenafi Kebede, *Roots of Black Music,* pp.50-53
32. Ibidem, pp.16-17
33. Yusef Ali, *The Music of the Moors in Spain,* in *Golden Age of the Moor,* ed Ivan Van Sertima, US, Transaction Publishers, 1992, pp.299, 305
34. Ibidem, pp.317-322
35. Ashenafi Kebede, *Roots of Black Music,* pp.12-15
36. Ibidem
37. Ibidem, pp.113-115
38. J. H. Kwabena Nketia, *The Music of Africa,* pp.135-138

## Chapter 2

39. Maulana Karenga, *Introduction to Black Studies, Third Edition,* US, University of Sankore Press, 2002, p.473
40. Implied in John Henrik Clarke ed, *Marcus Garvey and the Vision of Africa,* US, Vintage Books, 1970, p.18
41. Janheinz Jahn, *Muntu,* US, Grove Press, 1961, pp.187-190
42. Dizzy Gillespie, *To Be or Not to Bop,* UK, Quartet Books, 1979, pp.483-485
43. Ashenafi Kebede, *Roots of Black Music,* pp.129-130
44. Yosef A. A. Ben-Jochannan, *African Origins of the Major Western Religions,* US, Black Classic Press, 1970, pp.250-251
45. Maulana Karenga, *Introduction to Black Studies,* pp.474-475
46. Ashenafi Kebede, *Roots of Black Music,* p.133
47. J. H. Kwabena Nketia, *The Music of Africa,* pp.28-29 and A. Wiedmann, *Popular Literature in Ancient Egypt,* US, ECA Associates, 1990 (original 1902), pp.5-6
48. Ashenafi Kebede, *Roots of Black Music,* pp.130-131
49. *Sea shanty,* at http://en.wikipedia.org/wiki/Sea_shanty
50. Maulana Karenga, *Introduction to Black Studies,* p.475
51. Albert Murray, *Stomping the Blues,* US, Da Capo, 1976, pp.104-108
52. Ashenafi Kebede, *Roots of Black Music,* p.139
53. Carl Engel, *The Music of the Most Ancient Nations,* pp.259-263
54. For example the 'antiphonal' music of the sixteenth to eighteenth century masters Giovanni Gabrielli, Arcangelo Corelli, Henry Purcell, etcetera

55. Maulana Karenga, *Introduction to Black Studies*, pp.475-478
56. Eileen Southern, *The Music of Black Americans*, US, W. W. Norton, 1971, pp.249-251 and 401-4, Angela M. S. Nelson, *The Spiritual*, at https://www.christianhistoryinstitute.org/magazine/article/golden-age-of-hymns-spirituals/ and Robert Beckford, *The Gospel Truth*, Channel 4 television programme, 2005
57. Albert Murray, *Stomping the Blues*, pp.57-76
58. Ashenafi Kebede, *Roots of Black Music*, pp.139-40
59. Maulana Karenga, *Introduction to Black Studies*, pp.476-477
60. Ashenafi Kebede, *Roots of Black Music*, p.147
61. Ibidem, pp.146-147
62. See Robin Walker, *When We Ruled*, UK, Reklaw Education, 2013, p.59
63. See inside cover of Basil Davidson, *Africa: History of a Continent*, UK, Weidenfield & Nicholson, 1966 for sketch
64. See video: *Wynton Marsalis, Marsalis on Music, Volume 3*, Sony, Classic Film & Video, 1995
65. Maulana Karenga, *Introduction to Black Studies*, pp.478
66. Albert Murray, *Stomping the Blues*, p.140
67. Ibidem, p.144
68. Cf. ibidem, p.237
69. Ibidem, pp.230-244
70. Ibidem, p.238
71. Ibidem, p.170. See also video: *Wynton Marsalis, Blues & Swing*, CBS, 1988
72. Albert Murray, *Stomping the Blues*, pp.170-178
73. Dizzy Gillespie, *To Be or Not To Bop*, pp.483-485
74. Ibidem
75. Ian Carr, *Miles Davis*, UK, Paladin, 1984, p.26
76. Ibidem, pp.26-46

## Chapter 3

77. BBC television programme, *Dancing in the Streets: Whole Lotta Shakin'*, 1995
78. Ibidem
79. Albert Murray, *Stomping the Blues*, pp.30 and 40
80. Michael Rice, *Egypt's Making*, UK, Routledge, 1991, p.28
81. Sebastian Clarke, *Jah Music*, UK, Heinemann, 1980, pp.57-68
82. Ibidem, pp.96-97
83. BBC television programme, *Dancing in the Streets: Make It Funky*, 1995
84. For additional sidelines see television programme, *The James Brown Story*, Cable Communication Television, 1987
85. Leonard E. Barrett, *The Rastafarians*, US, Beacon Press, 1988, pp.215-216
86. BBC television programme, *Dancing in the Streets: Make It Funky*, 1995

87. BBC television programme, *Dancing in the Streets: Planet Rock,* 1995 and Channel 4 television programme, David Upshal, *The Hip Hop Years, Part 1,* RDF, 1999

88. BBC television programme, *Dancing in the Streets: Planet Rock,* 1995 and Channel 4 television programme, *Pump Up the Volume, Parts 1 and 2,* 2001. Note that according to this latter programme, House is older than Techno.

89. Sleeve notes to the album: Wynton Marsalis, *Black Codes (From the Underground),* US, CBS, 1985

# PART TWO

## EARLY BLACK LITERATURE

## INTRODUCTION

IN a 1958 text which was translated into English three years later, Janheinz Jahn, a German scholar, wrote the following: "Two essential cultural achievements were missing in the old Africa, however: architecture and writing."(1) To his credit, Mr Jahn partly atoned for this false statement when he issued the brilliant *Neo African Literature* a few years later. However, the idea that Africa has little or no early writings of its own is still the mainstream perspective. The idea that Africa has no impressive early architecture has been comprehensively destroyed by a number of other writers.

This essay, *Early Black Literature,* is designed to show that Africa does have early literary traditions. Moreover, the books and manuscripts still exist today.

In July 1913 the glorious Arthur Schomburg, then Secretary of the Negro Society for Historical Research, gave an address which was published as *Racial Integrity: A Plea for the Establishment of a Chair of Negro History in our Schools and Colleges, etc.* In the address, he described the Black literary tradition from Aesop, to the University of Timbuktu, through the likes of Juan Latino, Anthony William Amo, J. E. J. Capitein, Ignatius Sancho, Gustavus Vassa (i.e. Olaudah Equiano), Phillis Wheatley, Frances E. Watkins Harper, etcetera.(2) Still relevant reading today, I found this short essay of great inspiration.

Janheinz Jahn's *Neo African Literature* came out in Germany in 1966 and translated into English in 1968. It remains a powerful piece of research and scholarship. He includes nearly everyone mentioned above but also included other early literature probably unknown to Mr Schomburg. He included mediaeval Negro Arab writers, Old Hausa literature and Classical Swahili literature. He also included Black literature from all over the world written after 1913, the year of Schomburg's address.(3) This book remains unsurpassed but is now rare and out of print.

With the rediscovery of the mediaeval manuscripts of Timbuktu and elsewhere in Africa over the last few years, a remarkable publication came out of South Africa entitled *The Meanings of Timbuktu.* Edited by Professor

Shamil Jeppe and Professor Souleymane Bachir Diagne, the book contains essays on the early manuscripts of Timbuktu. They also included manuscripts from Hausaland, Sudan and the lands of the Swahili.(4) I have written about Timbuktu and its intellectual heritage elsewhere so I will not repeat that information here. The interested reader should consult *Everyday Life in an Early West African Empire* by Robin Walker, Siaf Millar and Saran Keita (UK, SIVEN, 2013).

The manuscripts and inscriptions of Ethiopia and the papyri and inscriptions of Egypt have been known to scholars for many years. However, neither have usually been included in discussions of Black writing and literature. This essay challenges this approach. Since the evidence is solid that both of these civilisations were originally Negro,(5) there is no valid reason to ignore this literary heritage.

This essay is in seven chapters. I begin with Ancient Egyptian literature. I introduce some of the Negro Arab writers. I discuss Ethiopian literature. I give a brief survey of Sudanese manuscripts. I survey Hausa manuscripts. I introduce Swahili literature. Finally, I introduce some of the early African American writers.

Read and enjoy!

Robin Walker

# CHAPTER 1: ANCIENT EGYPTIAN LITERATURE

The Ancient Egyptians left behind an impressive body of literary material. They wrote medical texts such as the *Edwin Smith* and *Ebers* Papyri. I have analysed some of the contents of these texts in *Blacks and Science Volume One*. They wrote mathematical texts such as the *Rhind, Berlin* and *Moscow* Mathematical Papyri. I have analysed some of the contents of these texts in *African Mathematics: History, Textbook and Classroom Lessons*. They wrote the *Pyramid Texts, Coffin Texts* and the *Coming Forth By Day*. Perhaps the most influential and profound body of literature in human history, I have analysed some of the contents of this material in *Blacks and Religion Volume One*. They also left behind documentary evidence of a more narrowly historical and political nature that allowed me to write a large portion of *When We Ruled*.

The Ancient Egyptians left behind other genres of literature that I shall describe below. They wrote wisdom teachings, apocalyptic material, stories and lyrical material.

The instruction, teaching, wisdom or philosophy texts cover moral and / or political philosophy and emphasise the importance of right doing for the individual and wise action for the political ruler for whom the text was written. They emphasise conformity to the main accepted idea of Ma'at. The best known of these texts is the *Maxims of Ptahhotep*.(6) Once considered the oldest complete book in world history, it dates back to the Fifth Dynasty period.(7)

The *Instruction of Kagemni* (like the *Maxims of Ptahhotep*) have survived on the *Prisse Papyrus,* a Twelfth Dynasty text. The *Teaching for Merykare* was written during the First Intermediate Period. The *Instruction of Amenemhet,* the *Instruction of Hardjedef,* and the *Loyalist Teaching* are Middle Kingdom texts. The *Instruction of Amenemope* is a New Kingdom compilation.(8) Professor Yosef ben-Jochannan, the great Ethiopian Egyptologist, points out that the authors of the Biblical book of *Proverbs* Chapter 22 copied whole passages from this text word-for-word.(9) To illustrate ben-Jochannan's ideas, I shall quote from a Wikipedia page entitled *Instruction of Amenemope:*

(Proverbs 22:17-18): "Incline thine ear, and hear the words of the wise, And apply thine heart to my doctrine; For it is pleasant if thou keep them in thy belly, that they may be established together upon thy lips" (Amenemope, ch. 1): "Give thine ear, and hear what I say, And apply thine heart to apprehend; It is good for thee to place them in thine heart, let them rest in the casket of thy belly; That they may act as a peg upon thy tongue"

(Proverbs 22:22): "Rob not the poor, for he is poor, neither oppress (or crush) the lowly in the gate." (Amenemope, ch. 2): "Beware of robbing the poor, and oppressing the afflicted."

(Proverbs 22:24-5): "Do not befriend the man of anger, Nor go with a wrathful man, Lest thou learn his ways and take a snare for thy soul." (Amenemope, ch. 10): "Associate not with a passionate man, Nor approach him for conversation; Leap not to cleave to such an one; That terror carry thee not away."

(Proverbs 22:29): "[if you] You see a man quick in his work, before kings will he stand, before cravens, he will not stand." (Amenemope, ch. 30): "A scribe who is skillful in his business findeth worthy to be a courtier"

(Proverbs 23:1): "When thou sittest to eat with a ruler, Consider diligently what is before thee; And put a knife to thy throat, If thou be a man given to appetite. Be not desirous of his dainties, for they are breads of falsehood." (Amenemope, ch. 23): "Eat not bread in the presence of a ruler, And lunge not forward(?) with thy mouth before a governor(?). When thou art replenished with that to which thou has no right, It is only a delight to thy spittle. Look upon the dish that is before thee, And let that (alone) supply thy need."

(Proverbs 23:4-5): "Toil not to become rich, And cease from dishonest gain; For wealth maketh to itself wings, Like an eagle that flieth heavenwards" (Amenemope, ch. 7): "Toil not after riches; If stolen goods are brought to thee, they remain not over night with thee. They have made themselves wings like geese. And have flown into the heavens."

(Proverbs 14:7): "Speak not in the hearing of a fool, for he will despise the wisdom of thy words" (Amenemope, ch. 21): "Empty not thine inmost soul to everyone, nor spoil (thereby) thine influence"

(Proverbs 23:10): "Remove not the widows landmark; And enter not into the field of the fatherless." (Amenemope, ch. 6): "Remove not the landmark from the bounds of the field ... and violate not the widows boundary"(10)

The inspiring story, *The Eloquent Peasant,* could also be considered an instructional work, but it depicts the individual hero as challenging unjust authority and breaking accepted norms in order to do so. The peasant stands up for his rights and makes eloquent and powerful arguments in court to get justice.(11)

The surviving narrative stories and tales are Middle and New Kingdom productions.

A number of Middle Kingdom examples are the *Tale of the Court of Pharaoh Khufu, Pharaoh Neferkare and General Sasenet, The Eloquent Peasant,* the *Story of Sinuhe,* and the *Story of the Shipwrecked Sailor.*(12) This last story is tale of an expedition to East Africa where the sailor is shipwrecked on a magical desert island. One of the characters he encounters is a talking serpent.(13)

Amongst the New Kingdom examples are the *Quarrel of Apepi and Seqenenre,* the *Taking of Joppa,* the *Tale of the Doomed Prince,* the *Tale of Two Brothers,* and the *Report of Wenamun.* Some of these stories concern Egyptian characters in foreign countries.(14)

The apocalyptic literature, lamentations or prophetic texts are thought to be of Middle Kingdom origin. These include the *Admonitions of Ipuwer,* the *Prophecy of Neferti,* and the *Dispute between a man and his Ba.*

The *Prophecy of Neferti* tells the story of Pharaoh Sneferu of the Fourth Dynasty summoning the sage and lector priest Neferti to his court. Neferti informs the king of a prophecy that the land will enter into a chaotic age, probably alluding to the First Intermediate Period, only to be restored to its former glory by a righteous king called Ameny. Since scholars believe that this was originally a Middle Kingdom text written during the time of a usurper ruler Amenemhet I, they see this document as pure political propaganda that implied that Ameny *is* Amenemhet I whose rule was foretold, and thus legitimated, by Neferti.(15)

The *Admonitions of Ipuwer* was a woe-doom text that describes the collapse of Egypt during the First Intermediate Period.(16) Alternative scholars, such as Immanuel Velikovsky, see it as the basis of the Ten Plagues story in the Bible.(17) To illustrate Velikovky's ideas, Ipuwer writes: "Nay, but the river is blood."(18) This is similar to *Exodus* 7:20 where it says: "all the waters that were in the river were turned to blood."

Ipuwer writes: "Doth a man drink therof, he rejecteth it as human, (for) one thirsteth for water."(19) This is similar to *Exodus* 7:21 where it says: "the river stank, and the Egyptians could not drink of the water of the river." Ipuwer writes: "and blood is everywhere".(20) This is similar to *Exodus* 7:21 where it says: "and there was blood throughout the land of Egypt." To give a final example, Ipuwer writes: "Nay, but all cattle, their hearts weep. The herds lament because of the land."(21) This is similar to *Exodus* 9:3 where it says: "Behold, the hand of the LORD is upon thy cattle which is in the field, upon the horses, upon the asses, upon the camels, upon the oxen, and upon the sheep: there shall be a very grievous murrain."

*Dispute between a man and his Ba* is a conversation between an individual with his *ba* (generally translated as soul) on whether it is better to continue living a tortured life or to choose death as an escape from melancholy.(22)

A number of poems, hymns and songs have survived from the early to the late periods.

The surviving hymns and songs from the Old Kingdom include the morning greeting hymns to the divine presence in their respective temples. These greetings begin with the repeated summons: "Awake in peace."(23)

There are songs dedicated to the Middle Kingdom ruler Senwosret III. They may be some of the earliest examples of the Praise Song genre of later African cultures. One such song has the following lyrics:

Praise to thee, Khakaure! Our Horus, Neter-kheperu!
That protecteth the land and extendeth his boundaries,
That vanquisheth the foreign countries with his crown.
That encloseth the Two Lands in his arms,
And (strangleth?) the foreign lands with his grip;
That slayeth the People of the Bow, with the stroke of the club.
Shooting of the arrow, or drawing of the string.
His might hath smitten the Troglodytes in their land,
And the fear of him hath slain the Nine Bows.
His slaughtering hath made thousands to die
Of the People of the Bow ..., that attacked his borders.
He that shooteth the arrow as doth Sekhmet,
When he overthroweth thousands of them that knew not his might.
It is the tongue of his majesty that confineth Nubia.
And it is his utterances that make the Bedouins to flee.
Sole youthful one that fighteth for his boundaries,
And suffereth not his people to wax faint;
That suffereth men to sleep unto daylight,
And his recruits to slumber, for his heart is their defender.

His decrees have made his boundaries,
And his word hath joined in one the Two River-banks.(24)

The New Kingdom ruler Thutmose III had an important poem inscribed on a stela erected at Karnak. In poetic verse, the stela commemorates his military victories over his enemies in which the divine forces give their blessings. Later Pharaohs, Seti I and Rameses II, reproduced the same poem on their monuments.(25) Poems were also written to honour divinities and even the Nile.

During the reign of Akhenaten the *Great Hymn to Aten* was written. Dedicated to Aten, the deity represented by the sun-disk, several writers have noticed the similarity between this *Hymn* and the contents of *Psalm* Chapter 104. Professor Théophile Obenga has praised the scientific content of this hymn. A passage in the hymn read as follows: 'Living sun disk, you who brought life into being ... trees and grass grows green ... your rays reach deep into the great green sea.' Professor Obenga noticed the link between sunlight giving life and the colour green. He believes that this is an early understanding of the concepts that we moderns would call photosynthesis and chlorophyll.(26)

A number of New Kingdom love songs have survived. Professor Adolf Erman compares the love songs to the *Song of Songs* in the Bible, citing the labels "sister" and "brother" that lovers used to address each other.(27) Here is the opening passage of one of them:

> [THE MAIDEN SPEAKS.] My brother, it is pleasant to go to the (pond) in order to bathe me in thy presence, that I may let thee see my beauty in my tunic of finest royal linen, it is wet ... I go down with thee into the water, and come forth again to thee ... Come and look at me.

> [THE YOUTH SPEAKS] The love of my sister is upon yonder side, a stretch of water is between (us both), and a crocodile waiteth on the sandbank. But when I go down into the water, I tread upon the flood; mine heart is courageous upon the waters ... and the water is like land to my feet. Her love, it is, that maketh me so strong.(28)

## CHAPTER 2: NEGRO ARAB LITERATURE

Lockman, also written as Luqman, was a semi legendary sage of the Arabian tradition. He was the original fable writer and was regarded by the Arabians as their greatest symbol of wisdom. There was an ironic saying in the early Near East "To teach wisdom to Lockman" which, as the great J. A. Rogers explains, is the equivalent of saying the equally ironic "Carrying coals to Newcastle."(29)

The Koran's Chapter XXXI is named after him. Verse 11 says: "And certainly we have bestowed the gift of wisdom on Lockman."(30)

Mr Rogers cites Claude-Étienne Savary, an Orientalist and translator of the Koran, as saying: "Most of the Arab writers agree that Lockman was a shepherd and that he was black with thick lips. The sky had given him eloquence and his precepts carried with them persuasion. They give to Lockman the same ingenious responses that are attributed to Esop, and describe him as having the same physical traits. If one adds to these points of resemblance those that are found in their works, one is led to believe that Esop and Lockman are one. Indeed the fables of Esop appear to be a copy of Lockman."(31)

Mr Rogers also cites the French savant Jean Joseph Marcel, editor of *Fables of Loqman,* as saying: "In effect, Lockman was Habechy, that is, an Abyssinian or Ethiopian slave, and the Oriental writers attribute to him nearly all the same physical characteristics that they give to Esop as well as the stories that we have of the life of this last-named famous fabulist."(32)

Mr Rogers taking his information from Al Masudi, the great Baghdad historian of the tenth century, says Lockman was a Nubian, slave of Lockain, son of Djesr and was born in the tenth year of King David's reign.(33) On this evidence, Rogers places Lockman around 1100 BC.

To cite Marcel once more: "all the Oriental writers, whether Arab or Persian, unite in agreeing that Lockman existed more than five centuries before the time of Esop ... In that case Lockman would have been the original."(34)

What were his most celebrated fables? I shall give a few examples:

أمثال لقمان الحكيم

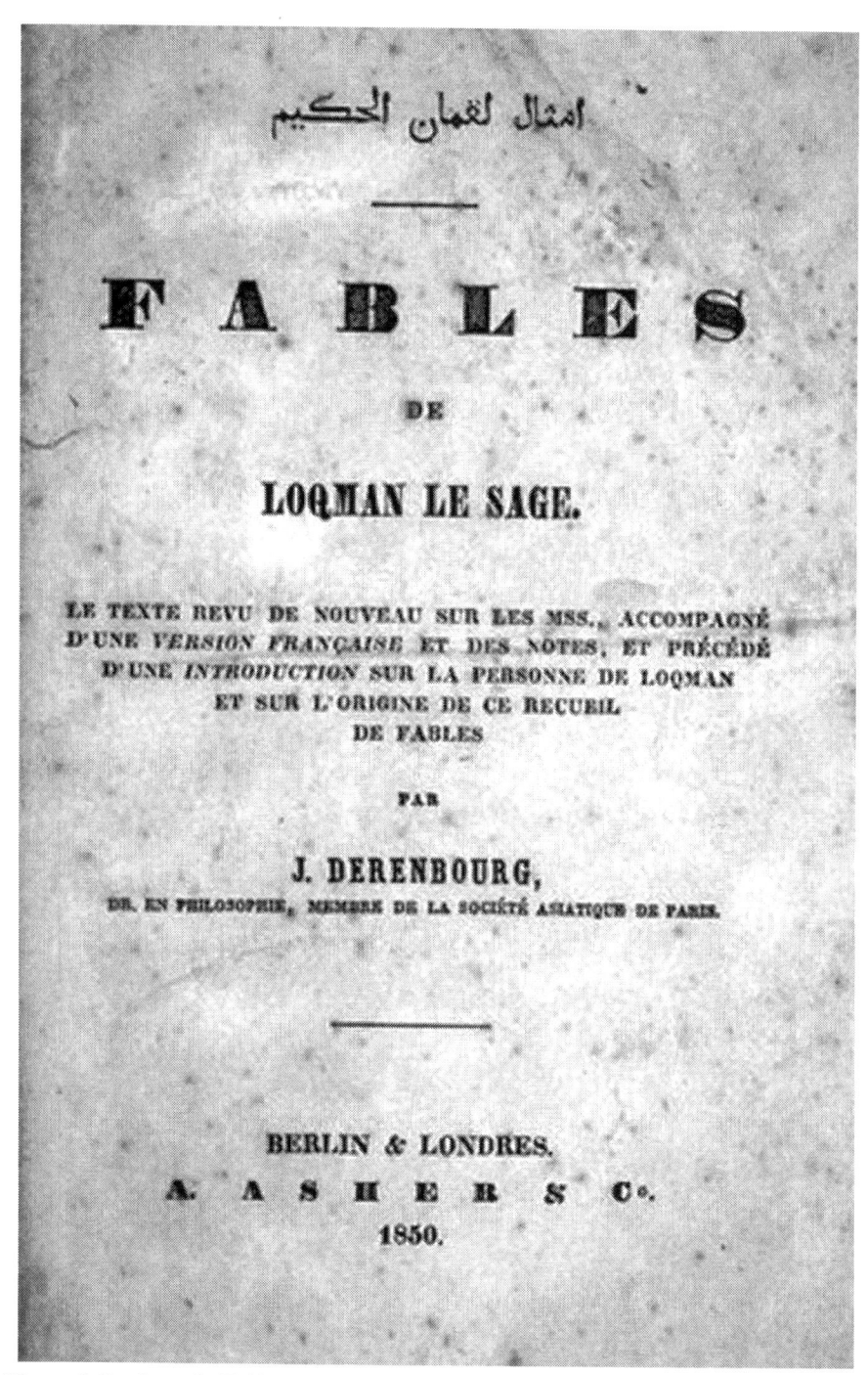

# FABLES

DE

## LOQMAN LE SAGE.

LE TEXTE REVU DE NOUVEAU SUR LES MSS., ACCOMPAGNÉ
D'UNE *VERSION FRANÇAISE* ET DES NOTES, ET PRÉCÉDÉ
D'UNE *INTRODUCTION* SUR LA PERSONNE DE LOQMAN
ET SUR L'ORIGINE DE CE RECUEIL
DE FABLES

PAR

J. DERENBOURG,

DR. EN PHILOSOPHIE, MEMBRE DE LA SOCIÉTÉ ASIATIQUE DE PARIS.

BERLIN & LONDRES.
A. ASHER & Cº.
1850.

Figure 1. Lockman's *Fables* have often been translated into European languages.

A fly buzzing around full of its own importance finally lit on the horns of the bull and said, "Let me know if I am too heavy for you and I will take myself off."

The bull replied, "Who are you? I did not know when you came nor shall I know when you leave."

A hare meeting a lioness one day said reproachfully, "I have always a great number of children while you have but one or two now and then."

The lioness replied, "It is true but my one child is a lion."

Finally:

A blacksmith had a dog that slept soundly while he was hammering at the forge, but as soon as he began eating the dog awoke. The master said, "O wicked dog, why does the sound of the hammer whose noise shakes the earth not trouble your sleep while the little noise I make in eating does?"(35)

Antar, also known as Antar Ibn Shaddad al Absi, was a poet and a soldier. Son of Zabiba, who scholars agree was a Black woman, there is disagreement over when he lived. Professor W. E. B. Du Bois suggests he was born around 498 AD. Janheinz Jahn and J. A. Rogers suggest he died in 615 AD. It is unlikely that all three were correct since he is said to have died on horseback in battle. It is difficult to imagine a man living to 117 years old let alone being so physically active!(36)

Runoko Rashidi, the leading African American historian, describes him as "considered by some to be the father of the codes of 'European' chivalry."(37) Mr Jahn says that he was a "poet whose place in Arabic literature is like Homer's in the West".(38) One of his poems was included as the sixth of the seven *Mo'allaqat* (Golden Odes), the pre-Islamic poetic masterpieces hung up from the Kaaba in Mecca so that pilgrims might do obeisance to them. The Russian composer Nikolai Rimsky-Korsakov wrote a symphony based on Antar's life.(39)

Finally, Richard Gottheil, a contributor to Charles Dudley Warner's *Library of the World's Best Literature: Volume 2,* says: "And even in the cities of the Orient to-day, the loungers in their cups can never weary of following the exploits of this black son of the desert, who in his person unites the great virtues of his people, magnanimity and bravery, with the gift of poetic speech. Its tone is elevated; its coarseness has as its origin the outspokenness of [an] unvarnished man; it does not peep through the thin veneer of licentious suggestiveness. It is never trivial, even in its long and wearisome descriptions, in its ever-recurring outbursts of love. Its language suits its thought: choice and educated."(40)

# Early Black Literature

His *Golden Ode* is an epic that sings his own praises, describes the beauties of nature, lauds victory on the battlefield, speaks highly of camels, but the biggest theme is love. One passage read as follows:

Thy heart, Antara, she did tear, those lips so sweet and chaste,
So ravishing a kiss they bear, so honey-sweet the taste.
When on thy lips I plant a kiss, O lovely damosel,
Thy mouth exudes a fragrant bliss like sweet musk perfume's smell.

Or like some pleasant garden's scent, with air of pure serene,
A peaceful place that few frequent and gentle rains keep green.
The morning clouds with showers abound, but frostless and benign,
That small round puddles in the ground like coins of silver shine.
Such copious rain the skies bestow, and every eve anew
The stream with nought to check its flow comes gushing swiftly through.(41)

Antar is also associated with a series of poems called the *Antar Romance*. Consisting of a thousand or more poems, Antar is known to have written some of them, but a school of devotees known as the 'Antarists' added more and more of their own verses in the same style. Asma'i, an eighth century philologist, collected and wrote them down. Abu Muwajjid Muhammad ibn al-Muhalla al-Antari produced an expanded version in the twelfth century. By the nineteenth century, a publisher in Arabia issued 32 volumes of the *Antar Romance*.(42)

Janheinz Jahn cites Joseph Hammer-Purgstall, a Viennese orientalist, as saying the following about the *Antar Romance:* "This is the work, and not, as is generally supposed, the *Thousand and One Nights,* which is the source of the stories which fill the tents and cottages in Arabia and Egypt."(43)

Finally, Janheinz Jahn cites W. A. Clouston, a British orientalist, as saying the following about the *Antar Romance:* "It is far from improbable that the famous Arabian Romance of Antar furnished the model for the earliest of the regular romances of chivalry which were current in Europe during the Middle Ages."(44)

Al Jahiz, also known as Al-Jahith, was a very important Black scholar of ninth century Baghdad. J. A. Rogers calls him the Lord of the Golden Age of Arab Literature and cites Christopher Dawson as saying: "Al-Jahiz was the greatest scholar and stylist of the ninth century."(45)

A prolific writer, his masterpiece was undoubtedly the seven volume *Book of Animals. The Telegraph,* a Conservative British daily broadsheet, carried an article which suggested why this book was of supreme importance.

'Next year, we will be celebrating the 200th anniversary of Charles Darwin's birth, and the 150th of the publication of his *On The Origin of Species,* which revolutionised our understanding of biology. But what if Darwin was beaten to the punch? Approximately 1,000 years before the British naturalist published his theory of evolution, a scientist working in Baghdad was thinking along similar lines. In the *Book of Animals,* abu Uthman al-Jahith (781-869), an intellectual of East African descent, was the first to speculate on the influence of the environment on species. He wrote: "Animals engage in a struggle for existence; for resources, to avoid being eaten and to breed. Environmental factors influence organisms to develop new characteristics to ensure survival, thus transforming into new species. Animals that survive to breed can pass on their successful characteristics to offspring." There is no doubt that it qualifies as a theory of natural selection.'(46)

Al-Jahiz also wrote *The Book of Eloquence and Rhetoric* which is still read widely today in Arab circles. Other important texts were *The Merit of the Turks, The Superiority of Speech to Silence, In Praise of Merchants and Dispraise of Officials* and *The Book of the Glory of the Blacks Over the Whites.*(47)

## CHAPTER 3: ETHIOPIAN LITERATURE

Ethiopia possesses a rich written tradition going back 2,500 years. The oldest surviving writings are inscriptions. The oldest of these date from 500 BC and continued to be inscribed as late as the ninth century AD. David Buxton, an authority on Ethiopian culture, suggests that these inscriptions were of historical and literary interest.(48)

The oldest are in Proto-Ethiopic, a script almost identical with Sabaean from Southern Arabia. Older writers like Mr Buxton saw this similarity as evidence that the culture of Ethiopia was not the product of Africans but the handiwork of colonists or invaders from Arabia!(49) Dr Peter Garlake pointed out that this same evidence could be used to argue the very reverse.

Figure 2. Ancient inscriptions in Proto-Ethiopic from Yeha. (Photo: Black Nine Films).

Figures 3 and 4. Important new information on the *Gospels of Abba Garima.*

It could be claimed that the culture of Southern Arabia was not the product of Arabians but the handiwork of colonists or invaders from Ethiopia!(50) Professor Roderick Grierson argues that it is possible to sit on the fence and suggests that Ethiopia and South Arabia developed a similar shared culture without necessarily arguing that one territory invaded and occupied the other.(51)

Later inscriptions written by Ethiopians from the early Christian Era are in the Greek language. Greek held the position as an international language much as English does today. Ethiopia also minted coins that had Greek language inscriptions on them.(52)

From the fourth century during the time of Emperor Ezana, the Ethiopians developed the Ethiopic script also called Ge'ez. This beautiful script influenced the Armenian and Georgian scripts of Eastern Europe.(53)

Ethiopia also possesses a rich literary heritage of books written on parchment. Scholars in relatively recent times have found that an Ethiopian manuscript, the *Gospels of Abba Garima,* may well be the oldest surviving illustrated Christian manuscript in world history dating from 330 to 650 AD (figures 3 and 4).(54)

Professor Richard Pankhurst, in a public lecture given in London, stated that Ethiopia possesses around 250,000 surviving manuscripts held in its old churches and monasteries. Others are in the National Library of Addis Ababa. In an essay, he calculates that at least another 5,000 manuscripts have been looted or acquired from Ethiopia and are held by European institutions and elsewhere all over the world.(55)

Mr Buxton states that amongst these manuscripts were books that contained biblical scriptures. Others were hagiographies of local or international saints. Others were theological and monastic texts. Some were royal court texts. There were religious hymns and verse. There were praise songs that honoured the great.(56) Otto Neugebauer states that there are also calendrical and astronomical texts. Professor Pankhurst states that there are also medical texts.

Ethiopian Bibles have books in them that are unknown or uncommon to many outside of the country such as the *Apocalypse of Esdra.* Moreover, the *Book of Jubilees, Book of Enoch* and *Ascension of Isaiah* only exist as complete texts in Ethiopic versions. Ethiopic Bibles also have additional books such as *The Testament of Our Lord, The Apostolic Decrees* and *The Apostolic Constitution.*(57)

Ethiopian scribes copied and translated texts from or about the African Desert Fathers. Thus there are Ethiopic translations of the *Lives* of St

Figure 5. The *Gunda Gunde Gospels*, with superb illustrations and written in the Ethiopic script, 1520.

Anthony and St Paul the Hermit. There are also Ethiopic translations of the highly important *Rule of St Pachomius,* the foundation text of all monastic living.(58)

According to Mr Buxton, the fourteenth and fifteenth centuries became the Great Age of Ethiopic Literature.(59) In his opinion, some of the popular writings were derived from foreign origins. He gives the examples of the three books associated with St George; his *Acts, Miracles* and *Praises.* Another such foreign work that became Ethiopianised was the *Miracles of the Virgin Mary.*(60)

The *Synaxarium* was a 4 volume corpus of saintly lore to be read in church on each and every day of the year. Each large volume covered a three month period. Beginning life as a translation of a Coptic text into Ethiopic in the late fourteenth century, the work gradually became Ethiopianised over the next hundred years enriched with the lives of local saints.(61)

The *Book of the Mysteries of Heaven and Earth* was a late fourteenth century book by a monk called Yeshaq inspired by a revelation from an angel. Containing complex and esoteric symbolism, the book likens the Virgin Mary to a single pearl of surpassing beauty.(62)

The *Acts of Abbot Philip* preserved the fearless denunciations that the Abbot made against the misdemeanours of Emperor Amda Tsion I (1314-44). In the opinion of Buxton, this work inspired other monks to record, reconstruct and even fabricate hagiographies of earlier holy men. Soon books appeared on the *Life* and the *Acts* of Tekla Haymanot. Other books appeared on the *Lives* of Abba Libanos, Abba Garima, Anna Pantaleone, Za-Mikael Aragawi, Yohannes Misraqawi, and Abuna Gabra Manfs Qiddus.(63)

The *Book of Light, Book of Humanity, Sword of the Trinity* and *Book of the Nativity* were written by scribes under the direction of Emperor Zar'a Yaqob (1434-68). The books denounce heresy and pagan practices with dire warnings and exhortations.(64)

David Buxton mentions the existence of hymns that date from the fourteenth century. Some of these narrate the Passion of Christ. Others tell the stories of the martyrs such as the massacre of the Christians by the Yemenites in 523 AD. They are in dialogue or in couplet forms.(65) Another collection of hymns are the *Deggwa* which are written using a form of musical notation. These hymns may be much older since they are said to have dated back to St Yared of Axum who lived in the sixth century.(66)

In the late fifteenth century the highly sophisticated *qené* form of poetry first appears. These were poems of two to eleven lines in length with a severely disciplined metrical structure. The aim was to give the maximum of cryptic thought with the minimum of words. The more ingeniously compact and obscure, the better. One group of these poems was the 'wax and gold' type. These poems had dual meanings. The 'wax' was the obvious meaning but the 'gold' represented the deeper meaning. These poems made full use of veiled allusions and puns. Originally these poems were sung in church. Later they were used to couch attacks on the powerful. Others were used to conceal messages of love.(67)

*Chronicle of the Wars of Amda Tsion I* is a lively document commended by scholars as a key source of Ethiopian history. The *Kebra Nagast* or Glory of Kings is considered the national epic of Ethiopia on which its national identity is built. This book tells the story of the Queen of Sheba, King Solomon, the Ark of the Covenant, etcetera. In addition, there are three sixteenth century chronicles of interest. *The Chronicle of Galawdewos* details the battles of Ethiopia against a Muslim invasion. The *History of the Conquests of Abyssinia* was an Islamic account of the same battles but probably written from the city of Harar by an Ethiopian Muslim.

Finally, there is the *History of the Gallas*. This work was written by a priest at the court of Malak Sagad.(68)

The *Fetha Negast* or Legislation of the Kings is the book that the Ethiopian kings used as their basis in law. Buxton claims that the precepts are based on Byzantine law and comes from an Arabic translation.(69)

Professor Otto Neugebauer, a historian of science, made a special study of Ethiopian calendrical and astronomical manuscripts dating from the fourteenth to the nineteenth centuries. Since they were copies of older manuscripts, Neugebauer could not give solid dates to the originals. There was one clear exception to this. Neugebauer explains: "It is, however, a singularly fortunate accident that we have an Ethiopic table that can be dated to the years Diocletian 27 to 85 (A. D. 311 to 369)." Some manuscripts show basic knowledge of the five planets (Mercury, Venus, Mars, Saturn and Jupiter). Some of these have diagrams of planetary periods. Others describe the 28 lunar mansions and include diagrams.(70)

Finally, Professor Pankhurst says Ethiopia possesses a small but important number of medical manuscripts. Written in Ge'ez and Amharic, these texts date from the second half of the eighteenth century. Others were from the nineteenth and early twentieth centuries. Broad in nature, the texts cover illnesses and diseases and their treatments. They also cover and combine issues of a magical nature such as averting the evil eye, overcoming evil spirits, defeating your enemies, etcetera. The scientific content of these texts describe treatments for epilepsy, fever, syphilis, rabies, skin diseases, kidney problems, haemorrhoids, constipation, diarrhoea, dysuria, itching, coughing, sterility and even snoring. The texts describe thousands of prescriptions that involved an extensive pharmacopeia derived from the vegetable, animal and mineral kingdoms.(71)

Early Black Literature        65

## CHAPTER 4: SUDANESE MANUSCRIPTS

The old Nubian Christian site of Qasr Ibrim has thousands of ecclesiastical documents in 8 different languages dating from the ninth to the eleventh centuries. They are in Meroitic, Old Nubian, Coptic, Greek Creole, Greek, Arabic, Latin and Turkish.(72) But as Professor Rex Sean O'Fahey laments: "they have yet to be published."(73)

According to the World Survey of Islamic Manuscripts, there are 30 surviving collections of old Sudanese manuscripts in Sudanese public and

Figure 6. The *Miracles of St Menas*, in the Old Nubian script, 1053 AD. (Photo: Robin Walker).

private collections. Of these, the oldest of the manuscripts identified dates to 1555 AD. The largest public collection is in the National Records Office in Khartoum. It houses 15,000 literary manuscripts. In addition, this institution has the archives of the Mahdist state that ruled in Sudan 1882 to 1898. This archive has an estimated 250,000 items. The University of Khartoum has around 3,000 manuscripts housed between several collections including a valuable collection of medical manuscripts. The University of Bergen in Norway has xerographic and photographic copies of 5,000 or more Sudanese manuscripts at their Centre for Middle Eastern and Islamic Studies.(74)

# CHAPTER 5: HAUSA LITERATURE

Professor Murray Last, a leading authority on Northern Nigerian history, estimates that in the year 1900, three years before the British colonisation of the region, there were 250,000 manuscripts in Northern Nigeria. Most were in private households and collections. Some huge collections were in the emir's palaces and scholarly households. He, himself, has catalogued 10,000 manuscripts in the National Archives in Kaduna and elsewhere in Northern Nigeria.(75)

The first major piece of Hausa literature was written in the late 1400s by Algerian cleric Sheikh Muhammad Al-Maghili. He taught Koranic studies in Katsina and law at Kano. The great Kano ruler Muhammad Rumfa commissioned him to write a treatise on government. Written in Arabic and entitled *On The Obligations of Princes,* an excerpt from this great work is given below:

> The sojourn of a prince in the city breeds all manner of trouble and harm. The bird of prey abides in open and wild places. Vigorous is the cock as he struts round his domains. The eagle can only win his realm by firm resolve, and the cock's voice is strong as he masters the hens. Ride, then, the horses of resolution upon the saddles of prudence. Cherish the land from the spoiling drought, from the raging wind, the dust-laden storm, the raucous thunder, the gleaming lightning, the shattering fireball and the beating rain. Kingdoms are held by the sword, not by delays. Can fear be thrust back except by causing fear? Allow only the nearest of your friends to bring you food and drink and bed and clothes. Do not part with your coat of mail and weapons and let no one approach you save men of trust and virtue. Never sleep in a place of peril. Have near to guard you at all times a band of faithful and gallant men, sentries, bowmen, horse and foot. Times of alarm are not like times of safety. Conceal your secrets from other people until you are master of your undertaking.(76)

The fall of Timbuktu in 1591 left Katsina the leading intellectual centre of West Africa. Abu Abdullah Muhammad ibn Muhammad (1595-1667), also called Dan Masani, was its most celebrated scholar. He wrote on law, theology, poetry, politics, and even on the wonders of Yorubaland.

Figure 7. Old manuscript in a Hausa collection in Kaduna.

Furthermore, he wrote a 500-page commentary on the *ishiriniya* of al-Fazzai, he also wrote a treatise on rebellion, and one on Maliki law.(77) Muhammad ibn Muhammad, an astronomer and mathematician, wrote an interesting paper on the mathematical problem of magic squares.(78) I discuss this mathematics problem in my book (co-written with John Matthews) called *African Mathematics: History, Textbook and Classroom Lessons* (UK, Reklaw Education, 2014, pp.75-81).

Manuscripts in the Hausa and Fulfulde languages began to appear in the seventeenth century. John Phillips mentions a seventeenth century Hausa manuscript by a Kano scholar in the Jos Museum manuscript collection.(79) Dr Hamid Bobboyi mentions a surviving Arabic translation of a Fulfulde text by a scholar called al-Fallati who flourished between 1688 and 89.(80)

The Sokoto Caliphate ruled the Northern Nigeria region from 1804 to 1904. The founders of this state were Sheikh Uthman Dan Fodio (1754-1817), his brother Sheikh Abdullahi (d.1829), and his son Muhammad Bello (d.1837). These radicals were men of impressive intellects. Earlier scholars, like Dr Basil Davidson reported that they wrote 258 books, essays and articles between them. Most of their writings were in Arabic but a significant number of manuscripts were in local languages, mainly Hausa

# Early Black Literature

and Fulfulde. Their successors also made significant contributions to knowledge. However, Professor Last claims that the three Sokoto scholars actually wrote over 300 prose works and points out that another erudite contemporary Abd al-Qadar b. Al-Mustafa wrote 48 works on secular subjects.(81)

To give some examples, Sheikh Uthman Dan Fodio wrote a number of poems in Fulfulde to warn the masses on the need for a religious reformation. His *Ills of Hausaland* describes the ungodly evil in Hausa society and the complicit silence of the ruling class. His *Advice* warns the people of the need to restrict social contact with oppressive rulers and instead keep company with the pious. He wrote poems in Hausa also. His *The Miserable World* shows the ephemeral nature of the world and argues that it is only the afterlife that is permanent. His *Mother of Poems* is a poem calling for repentance.(82)

Nana Asma'u, the daughter of Uthman Dan Fodio, wrote a poem called *The Qur'an*. Composed and translated in Arabic, Fulfulde and Hausa, it compresses the holy book into 30 verses with the names of every chapter of the Qur'an. This was a work of great pedagogical value.(83) She also wrote *The Way of the Pious, The Path of Truth, Signs of the Day of Judgement, Fear This, Elegy for Halima, Medicine of the Prophet, The Journey, Be Sure of God's Truth,* etcetera.(84)

Janheinz Jahn explains the types and structure of Hausa poetry as it probably existed in the nineteenth century. Professional poets were also singers who often performed with musicians. Some performed for certain wealthy households. Others were wandering minstrels who, with their troupe, gave recitals to different audiences. The poetry that they read or sang came from two sets of inspirations, religious or secular sources. The religious poetry was written by Mallams or other holy individuals. It was written down and followed classical Arabic metres. The non-religious material was often unwritten, used non Arabic metres, and consisted of three types of poem or song--the praise song (*yabo*), the lampoon (*zambo*) or the love song (*bege*).(85) However Professor Last points out that one pornographic poem from the nineteenth century survived in the Emir of Kano's collection(86) and it was written down!

Mr Jahn gave the following example of a humorous secular Hausa poem collected between 1904 and 1914.

> The master would welcome me in,
>   But the miserable dog only growls.
>  His legs are so spindly thin,

   Like a quiver of arrows he jowls.
I've heard of the misers who won't spend a bean
   But never met anyone mangy and mean
Like this mastiff you meet at the door,
   Son of sin and the son of a whore.
You can eat almost all other animal's meat,
   But you, you damned dog, no one ever would eat.
Barking's the only real skill you can claim.
   You poisonous creature, we'd hate you as game.(87)

# CHAPTER 6: SWAHILI LITERATURE

Swahili is the most widely spoken language in Africa. Some 4,000 old manuscripts are preserved at the University of Dar es Salaam at their Institute of Kiswahili Research. There are collections totalling over 600 manuscripts in Zanzibar in the Museums, Archives and the Antiquities departments. There are also Swahili manuscripts in Germany and in London.(88)

The importance of the Swahili literary tradition was well explained by Professor Rex Sean O'Fahey who said: "Swahili is also the Islamic African language with the most highly developed literary tradition, inviting comparison, particularly in regard to its poetry, with Farsi (Iran), Urdu (India) and Turkish."(89)

The oldest surviving Swahili manuscripts date from the seventeenth century but its poetry tradition is much older. There are three major classical Swahili poetic forms; the *tendi, nyimbo* and the *shari*. The poems were oral or written. Some were sung. The Swahili poetry tradition, judging from linguistic grounds, dates back to pre-Islamic times. The *Fumo Liongo* poetry cycle probably dates from the thirteenth or fourteenth centuries. A cultural hero from the Northern Kenyan coast, Fumo Liongo could have lived at any time from the seventh to the seventeenth century. He is said to have begun this cycle of poems and others have added to it.(90) The basic story of the epic is Fumo Liongo's struggle with Daudi Mringwari, the Sultan of Pate who was Liongo's maternal cousin. Mringwari viewed the poet as a potential usurper to his throne while Liongo was convinced that he was the rightful heir to the kingdom. Thus the succession to the throne of the Pate city state forms the core of the story.(91)

| | |
|---|---|
| Kimo kawa mtukufu | He was of glorious stature |
| Mpana sana mrefu | Very broad and tall |
| Majimbo kawa maarufu | He became famous in the countryside |
| Watu huja kwangaliya | And people came to look at him |
| | |
| Ni mwanamume sahihi | He was a real man |
| Kama simba una zihi | Strong as a lion |

**Figure 8.** Swahili astronomical texts from the Jumba La Mtwana Museum, Kenya (Photo: Robin Walker).

| | |
|---|---|
| Usiku na asubuhi | Be it night or day |
| Kutembea ni mamoja | He freely moved about |
| | |
| Ghafla kikutokeya | If he suddenly appeared to you |
| Mkojo hukupoteya | You would wet yourself with fright |
| Tapo likakuiliya | You would start trembling |
| Ukatapa na kuliya | You would tremble as you cry out(92) |

The Swahili Epics or *tendi* are often of 5,000 quatrains or more in length. The longest known *tendi* is 45,000 quatrains and concerns the last moments of the Prophet Mahomet. The subject matter of these epics are themes from Islamic history. However, most Swahili poetry concerns secular themes but there was always more effort to preserve the religious material for posterity. Some 300 *tendi* from the eighteenth to the twentieth centuries are known. Unfortunately only 6 of these have been edited or translated.(93)

Of the manuscripts, the oldest surviving Swahili text is a 1652 document by Bwana Mwengo called *Epic of Hamziyya*. Written in the Swahili city state of Pate, it is a Swahili rendering of a popular Arabic text. Another surviving document is the *Epic of Heraclitus* (also called the *Epic of Tabuka*) of 1728 or 9.(94) The *Epic of Heraclitus* recounts numerous events of the Byzantine-Arab Wars and the Byzantine-Ottoman Wars. The Byzantine ruler at the beginning was Heraclitus. The epic story covers a period from 628 with the Battle of Mu'tah, to 1453 with the Fall of

Constantinople. Incidentally, "Tabuka" is the Swahili rendering of Tabuk, a city in Saudi Arabia.(95)

*The Soul's Awakening* by Ali Bin Nassir (1720-1820) is possibly the greatest of the known works in the *tendi* form from the eighteenth century. It ends as follows:

| | |
|---|---|
| Sasa takhitimu tatia tama | I will now end here and put a stop |
| atakofuata na kuyandama | Whoever shall heed these words and stick to them |
| tapata khatima na mwisho mwema | Will be blessed till his or her life's end |
| Rabbi hukuomba, tujaaliye | May God Almighy grant us this prayer |
| | |
| Rabbi mrahimu mwenye kutunga | May the Lord shower blessings upon the composer |
| na mezokhitimu, mja malenga | And the poet who has brought the work to an end |
| Sala na salamu ni zao kinga | May God's blessings and peace be their shield |
| Rabbi takabali ziwashukiye | May your Divine care be upon them(96) |

In the nineteenth century, the *shari* form of poetry appeared. The material was intimate, dialogic and polemical. Composed for particular occasions, the Swahili poems in the London and Berlin collections are primarily in this genre.(97)

Finally, it is worth noting that the Zanzibar collections have eighteenth and nineteenth century texts that contain medical information. One such book *The Tree of the Throne* describes roots, plants and herbs that can be used for medicinal purposes as well as magic. Other manuscripts deal with astronomy and navigation.(98)

# CHAPTER 7: AFRICAN AMERICAN LITERATURE

Lucy Terry (*c*.1730-1821) is the author of the earliest known work of literature by an African American. She was captured in Africa and was subsequently enslaved by Ebenezer Wells of Deerfield. Her ballad-poem *Bars Fight* colourfully and starkly describes a Native American raid on the European colonisers of Deerfield:(99)

> August 'twas the twenty-fifth,
> Seventeen hundred forty-six;
> The Indians did in ambush lay,
> Some very valiant men to slay,
> The names of whom I'll not leave out.
> Samuel Allen like a hero fought,
> And though he was so brave and bold,
> His face no more shalt we behold
> Eleazer Hawks was killed outright,
> Before he had time to fight,
> Before he did the Indians see,
> Was shot and killed immediately.
> Oliver Amsden he was slain,
> Which caused his friends much grief and pain.
> Simeon Amsden they found dead,
> Not many rods distant from his head.
> Adonijah Gillett we do hear
> Did lose his life which was so dear.
> John Sadler fled across the water,
> And thus escaped the dreadful slaughter.
> Eunice Allen see the Indians coming,
> And hopes to save herself by running,
> And had not her petticoats stopped her,
> The awful creatures had not catched her,
> Nor tommy hawked her on the head,
> And left her on the ground for dead.
> Young Samuel Allen, Oh! lack-a-day!
> Was taken and carried to Canada.(100)

Phillis Wheatley (*c*.1753-1784) was the next important African American

**Early Black Literature** 75

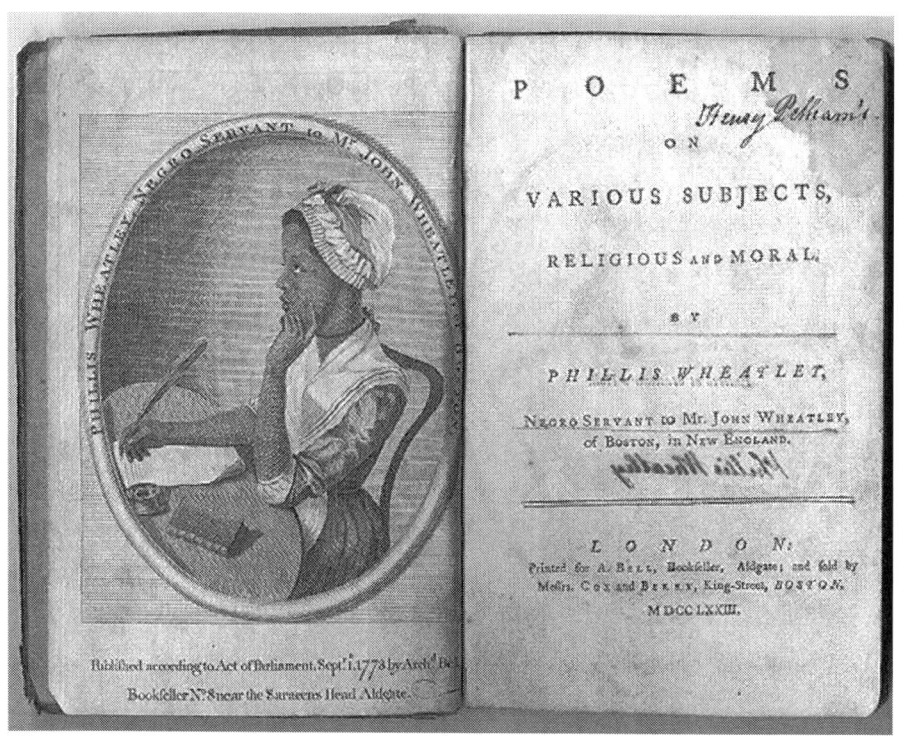

Figure 9. Phillis Wheatley's, *Poems on Various Subjects, Religious and Moral*, 1773.

poet. Born in Senegal, she was sold into slavery at the age of seven and transported to North America. She was purchased and enslaved by the Wheatley family of Boston. They taught her to read in English, which she mastered in sixteen months, and encouraged her poetry when they saw her talent. She also gained some proficiency in Latin. Influenced by Alexander Pope, and rich with Biblical and solar deity influences, she published *Poems on Various Subjects, Religious and Moral* (1773). This brought her fame both in England and the American colonies.(101) Wikipedia says this publication ultimately made her "the most famous African on the face of the earth." Even figures such as George Washington and Voltaire praised her work.(102)

The collection included poems with the following titles: *On Virtue, To the University of Cambridge, in New England, To the King's Most Excellent Majesty, On the Death of a young Lady of five Years of Age,* etcetera. However, there is a redeemed by Christianity theme running through some of her poems. This was also true of most of the eighteenth century Black

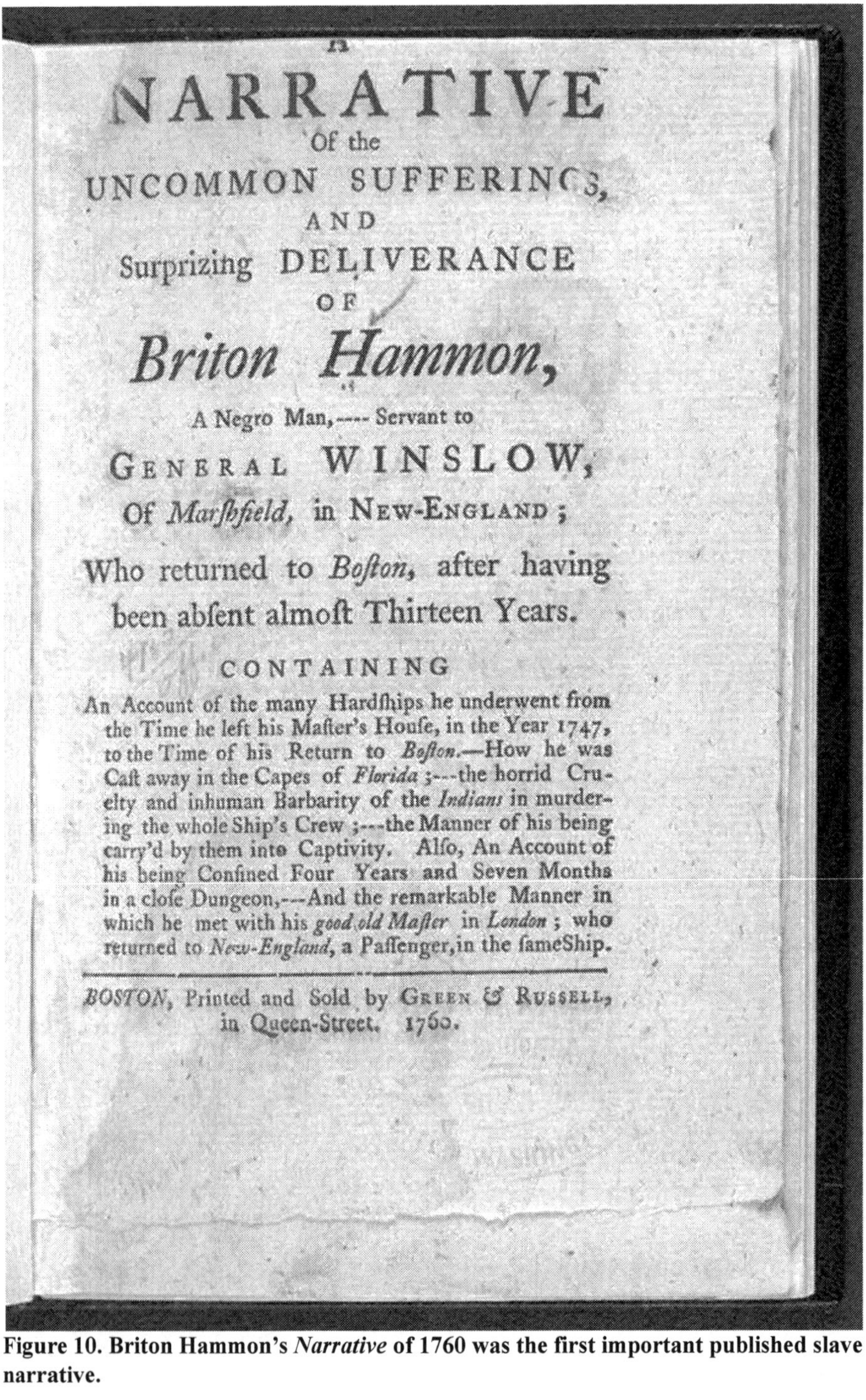

# NARRATIVE

Of the

## UNCOMMON SUFFERINGS,

AND

Surprizing DELIVERANCE

OF

## Briton Hammon,

A Negro Man,---- Servant to

### GENERAL WINSLOW,

Of *Marshfield*, in NEW-ENGLAND;

Who returned to *Boston*, after having been absent almost Thirteen Years.

CONTAINING

An Account of the many Hardships he underwent from the Time he left his Master's House, in the Year 1747, to the Time of his Return to *Boston*.—How he was Cast away in the Capes of *Florida*;---the horrid Cruelty and inhuman Barbarity of the *Indians* in murdering the whole Ship's Crew;---the Manner of his being carry'd by them into Captivity. Also, An Account of his being Confined Four Years and Seven Months in a close Dungeon,---And the remarkable Manner in which he met with his *good old Master* in *London*; who returned to *New-England*, a Passenger, in the sameShip.

BOSTON, Printed and Sold by GREEN & RUSSELL, in Queen-Street. 1760.

Figure 10. Briton Hammon's *Narrative* of 1760 was the first important published slave narrative.

# Early Black Literature

writers. A good example is *On being brought from Africa to America:*

'Twas mercy brought me from my *Pagan* land,
Taught my benighted soul to understand
That there's a God, that there's a *Saviour* too:
Once I redemption neither sought nor knew.
Some view our sable race with scornful eye,
"Their colour is a diabolic dye."
Remember, *Christians, Negroes,* black as *Cain,*
May be refin'd, and join th' angelic train.(103)

Beginning with Briton Hammon's *Narrative of the uncommon sufferings, and surprizing deliverance of Briton Hammon,* published in Boston, 1760, a new genre was born. Enslaved Africans told their experiences of enslavement. Ukawsaw Gronniosaw wrote *A Narrative of the Most Remarkable Particulars in the Life of James Albert "Ukawsaw Gronniosaw", an African Prince,* published in London, 1772. Olaudah Equiano wrote, *The Interesting Narrative and the life of "Olaudah Equiano" or Gustavus Vassa, the African,* also published in London, 1789. There was also Venture Smith's book *A Narrative of the Life and Adventures of Venture, a Native of Africa: But Resident Above Sixty Years in the United States of America,* this time published in New London, 1798.(104)

The African American novel was born in 1853 with *Clotel, or The President's Daughter.* Written by William Wells Brown, a runaway slave, the book was published in London. The novel tells the story of Clotel and her sister who were fictional slave daughters of Thomas Jefferson. It explores how enslavement destroyed African American families and the particular challenges faced by mulattoes. Featuring Currer, an enslaved mixed-race woman, and her daughters Althesa and Clotel, fathered by Thomas Jefferson, their comfortable lives end after Jefferson's death. They had to address many hardships, with the women taking heroic action to preserve their families.

Brown also wrote the *Narrative of William W. Brown, a Fugitive Slave, Written by Himself.* He wrote a play after his return to the United States from Europe: *The Escape; or, A Leap for Freedom* (1858). He read the latter aloud at abolitionist meetings in lieu of the typical lecture. Finally, he wrote several histories, including *The Black Man: His Antecedents, His Genius, and His Achievements* (1863); *The Negro in the American Rebellion* (1867), considered the first historical work about Black soldiers

**Figure 11. Frances Ellen Watkins Harper (1825-1911).**

in the American Revolutionary War; and *The Rising Son* (1873). His last book was another memoir, *My Southern Home* (1880).(105)

Frances Ellen Watkins Harper (1825-1911) wrote stories, novels and poems bristling with emotion and heroism. Her first volume of verse, *Forest Leaves* was published in 1845 when she was 20. Her second book,

*Poems on Miscellaneous Subjects* (1854), was even more popular. The two volumes sold over 50,000 copies.(106) One of the poems published was *The Slave Auction.*

> The sale began--young girls were there,
>   Defenceless in their wretchedness.
> Whose stifled sobs of deep despair
>   Revealed their anguish and distress.
>
> And mothers stood with streaming eyes,
>   And saw their dearest children sold;
> Unheeded rose their bitter cries,
>   While tyrants bartered them for gold.
>
> And woman, with her love and truth--
>   For these in sable forms may dwell--
> Gaz'd on the husband of her youth,
>   With anguish none may paint or tell.
>
> And men, whose sole crime was their hue,
>   The impress of their Maker's hand,
> And frail and shrinking children, too.
>   Were gathered in that mournful band.
>
> Ye who have laid your love to rest,
>   And wept above their lifeless clay.
> Know not the anguish of that breast.
>   Whose lov'd are rudely torn away.
>
> Ye may not know how desolate
>   Are bosoms rudely forced to part.
> And how a dull and heavy weight
>   Will press the life-drops from the heart.

In 1859 her story *The Two Offers* was published in *Anglo-African Magazine*. She continued to publish poetry and short stories. However, she was best known for the novel, *Iola Leroy, or Shadows Uplifted* (1892), published when she was 67.(107) Arthur Schomburg quotes Mr J. J. Thomas, author of *Creole Grammar* as saying the following about Harper: "But it is as a poet that posterity will hail her in the coming ages of our race; for pathos, depth of spiritual insight, and magical exercise of a rare power of self utterance, it will hardly be questioned that she has surpassed every competitor among females--white or black--save and except Elizabeth

Barrett Browning, with whom the gifted African stands on much the same plane of poetic excellence."(108)

Frank J. Webb (1828-1894) was a novelist, poet, and essayist from Philadelphia, Pennsylvania. His novel, *The Garies and Their Friends* (1857), was the second novel by an African American to be published. Concentrating on the daily lives of free Blacks in the North, it was published in London. Webb and his wife soon moved to Jamaica, and he lived there for 10 years after her death, not returning to the United States until 1869.(109) Noted for its raw and uncompromising depiction of an anti-Black race riot with full menace, here is an excerpt from Chapter XX of the novel:

They all returned to their chairs by the drawing-room fire after this occurrence, and remained in comparative silence for some time, until loud cries of "Fire! fire!" startled them from their seats.

"The whole of the lower part of the city appears to be in a blaze," exclaimed one of the party who had hastened to the window; "look at the flames--they are ascending from several places. They are at their work; we may expect them here soon."

"Well, they'll find us prepared when they do come," rejoined Mr. Walters.

"What do you propose?" asked Mr. Ellis. "Are we to fire on them at once, or wait for their attack?"

"Wait for their attack, by all means," said he, in reply;--"if they throw stones, you'll find plenty in that room with which to return the compliment; if they resort to fire-arms, then we will do the same; I want to be strictly on the defensive--but at the same time we must defend ourselves fully and energetically."

In about an hour after this conversation a dull roar was heard in the distance, which grew louder and nearer every moment.

"Hist!" said Esther; "do you hear that noise? Listen! isn't that the mob coming?"

Mr. Walters opened the shutter, and then the sound became more distinct. On they came, nearer and nearer, until the noise of their voices became almost deafening.

There was something awful in the appearance of the motley crowd that, like a torrent, foamed and surged through the streets. Some were bearing large pine torches that filled the air with thick smoke and partially lighted up the surrounding gloom. Most of them were armed with clubs, and a few with guns and pistols.

As they approached the house, there seemed to be a sort of consultation between the ringleaders, for soon after every light was extinguished, and the deafening yells of "Kill the niggers!" "Down with the Abolitionists!" were almost entirely stilled.

"I wonder what that means," said Mr. Walters, who had closed the shutter, and was surveying, through an aperture that had been cut, the turbulent mass below. "Look out for something soon."

He had scarcely finished speaking, when a voice in the street cried, "One--two--three!" and immediately there followed a volley of missiles, crushing in the windows of the chamber above, and rattling upon the shutters of the room in which the party of defenders were gathered. A yell then went up from the mob, followed by another shower of stones.

"It is now our turn," said Mr. Walters, coolly. "Four of you place yourselves at the windows of the adjoining room; the rest remain here. When you see a bright light reflected on the crowd below, throw open the shutters, and hurl down stones as long as the light is shining. Now, take your places, and as soon as you are prepared stamp upon the floor."

Each of the men now armed themselves with two or more of the largest stones they could find, from the heap that had been provided for the occasion; and in a few seconds a loud stamping upon the floor informed Mr. Walters that all was ready. He now opened the aperture in the shutter, and placed therein a powerful reflecting light which brought the shouting crowd below clearly into view, and in an instant a shower of heavy stones came crashing down upon their upturned faces.

Yells of rage and agony ascended from the throng, who, not seeing any previous signs of life in the house, had no anticipation of so prompt and severe a response to their attack. For a time they swayed to and fro, bewildered by the intense light and crushing shower of stones that had so suddenly fallen upon them. Those in the rear, however, pressing forward, did not permit the most exposed to retire out of reach of missiles from the house; on perceiving which, Mr. Walters again turned the light upon them, and immediately another stony shower came rattling down, which caused a precipitate retreat.

"The house is full of niggers!--the house is full of niggers!" cried several voices--"Shoot them! kill them!" and immediately several shots were fired at the window by the mob below.

"Don't fire yet," said Mr. Walters to one of the young men who had his hand upon a gun. "Stop awhile. When we do fire, let it be to some purpose--let us make sure that some one is hit."

Whilst they were talking, two or three bullets pierced the shutters, and flattened themselves upon the ceiling above.

"Those are rifle bullets," remarked one of the young men--"do let us fire."

"It is too great a risk to approach the windows at present; keep quiet for a little while; and, when the light is shown again, fire. But, hark!" continued he, "they are trying to burst open the door. We can't reach them there without exposing ourselves, and if they should get into the entry it would be hard work to dislodge them."

"Let us give them a round; probably it will disperse those farthest off--and those at the door will follow," suggested one of the young men.

"We'll try it, at any rate," replied Walters. "Take your places, don't fire until I show the light--then pick your man, and let him have it. There is no use to fire, you know, unless you hit somebody. Are you ready?" he asked.

"Yes," was the prompt reply.

"Then here goes," said he, turning the light upon the crowd below--who, having some experience in what would follow, did their best to get out of reach; but they were too late--for the appearance of the light was followed by the instantaneous report of several guns which did fearful execution amidst the throng of ruffians. Two or three fell on the spot, and were carried off by their comrades with fearful execrations.

Figure 12. Paul Laurence Dunbar (1872-1906).

Finally, the last writer that I shall discuss is Paul Laurence Dunbar (1872-1906). He was a poet, novelist, and playwright. Beginning to write poetry as a child, he published his first poems at the age of 16 in a local newspaper. His more popular work was written in an African American dialect typically associated with the South. He also wrote in conventional American English in other poetry and novels.(110) I shall end this section with two of his best known poems. Firstly, here is the opening of *Chrismus On The Plantation:*

It was Chrismus Eve, I mind hit fu' a mighty gloomy day--
Bofe de weathah an' de people--not a one of us was gay;
Cose you'll t'ink dat's mighty funny 'twell I try to mek hit cleah,
Fu' a da'ky's allus happy when de holidays is neah.

But we wasn't, fu' dat mo'nin' Mastah'd tol' us we mus' go,
He'd been payin' us sence freedom, but he couldn't pay no mo';
He wa'n't nevah used to plannin' 'fo' he got so po' an' ol',
So he gwine to give up tryin', an' de homestead mus' be sol'.

I kin see him stan'in' now erpon de step ez cleah ez day,
Wid de win' a-kind o' fondlin' thoo his haih all thin an' gray;
An' I 'membah how he trimbled when he said, "It's ha'd fu' me,
Not to mek yo' Chrismus brightah, but I 'low it wa'n't to be."

All de women was a-cryin', an' de men, too, on de sly,
An' I noticed somep'n shinin' even in ol' Mastah's eye.
But we all stood still to listen ez ol' Ben come f'om de crowd
An' spoke up, a-try'n' to steady down his voice and mek it loud:--

The final example is his *Ode To Ethiopia:*

O Mother Race! to thee I bring
This pledge of faith unwavering,
  This tribute to thy glory.
I know the pangs which thou didst feel,
When Slavery crushed thee with its heel,
  With thy dear blood all gory.

Sad days were those--ah, sad indeed!
But through the land the fruitful seed
  Of better times was growing.
The plant of freedom upward sprung,
And spread its leaves so fresh and young--
  Its blossoms now are blowing.

On every hand in this fair land,
Proud Ethiope's swarthy children stand
  Beside their fairer neighbor;
The forests flee before their stroke,
Their hammers ring, their forges smoke,--
  They stir in honest labour.

They tread the fields where honour calls;
Their voices sound through senate halls
  In majesty and power.
To right they cling; the hymns they sing
Up to the skies in beauty ring,
  And bolder grow each hour.

Be proud, my Race, in mind and soul;
Thy name is writ on Glory's scroll
  In characters of fire.
High 'mid the clouds of Fame's bright sky
Thy banner's blazoned folds now fly,
  And truth shall lift them higher.

Thou hast the right to noble pride,
Whose spotless robes were purified
  By blood's severe baptism.
Upon thy brow the cross was laid,
And labour's painful sweat-beads made
  A consecrating chrism.

No other race, or white or black,
When bound as thou wert, to the rack,
  So seldom stooped to grieving;
No other race, when free again,
Forgot the past and proved them men
  So noble in forgiving.

Go on and up! Our souls and eyes
Shall follow thy continuous rise;
  Our ears shall list thy story
From bards who from thy root shall spring,
And proudly tune their lyres to sing
  Of Ethiopia's glory.

## NOTES AND REFERENCES

### Introduction

1. Janheinz Jahn, *Muntu,* US, Grove Press, 1961, p.185
2. Arthur Schomburg, *Racial Integrity: A Plea for the Establishment of a Chair of Negro History in our Schools and Colleges, etc,* US, Black Classic Press reprint, 1913
3. Janheinz Jahn, *Neo-African Literature,* US, Grove Press, 1968
4. Shamil Jeppe and Souleymane Bachir Diagne eds, *The Meanings of Timbuktu,* South Africa, HSRC, 2008
5. Robin Walker, *When We Ruled,* UK, Reklaw Education, 2013, pp.117-132, 143-153, 317-345, 526-528, 679-683

### Chapter 1

6. Adolf Erman, *The Literature of the Ancient Egyptians,* UK, Methuen & Co., 1927, pp.54-65
7. Isaac Meyer, *Oldest Books in the World,* UK, Kegan Paul, Trench, Trubner & Co., 1900
8. *Ancient Egyptian literature,* at http://en.wikipedia.org/wiki/Ancient_Egyptian_literature
9. Yosef A. A. ben-Jochannan, *African Origin of the Major Western Religions,* US, Black Classic Press, 1970, pp.164-5
10. *Instruction of Amenemope,* at http://en.wikipedia.org/wiki/Instruction_of_Amenemope
11. Adolf Erman, *The Literature of the Ancient Egyptians,* pp.116-131
12. *Ancient Egyptian literature,* at http://en.wikipedia.org/wiki/Ancient_Egyptian_literature
13. Adolf Erman, *The Literature of the Ancient Egyptians,* pp.29-35
14. *Ancient Egyptian literature,* at http://en.wikipedia.org/wiki/Ancient_Egyptian_literature
15. Cf. Asa G. Hilliard III, *Waset, The Eye of Ra and the Abode of Maat: The Pinnacle of Black Leadership in the Ancient World,* in *Egypt Revisited,* ed Ivan Van Sertima, US, Transaction Publishers, 1989, pp.217-8
16. Adolf Erman, *The Literature of the Ancient Egyptians,* pp.92-108
17. Frances Hitchin, *The World Atlas of Mysteries,* UK, Book Club Associates, 1978, p.173
18. Quoted in Adolf Erman, *The Literature of the Ancient Egyptians,* p.95

19. Ibidem
20. Ibidem
21. Ibidem, p.98
22. Ibidem, pp.86-92
23. Ibidem, pp.12-3
24. Quoted in ibidem, pp.134-5
25. Ibidem, pp.254-8
26. Théophile Obenga, *African Philosophy: The Pharaonic Period 2780-330 BC*, Senegal, Per Ankh, 2004, pp.91-113
27. Adolf Erman, *The Literature of the Ancient Egyptians*, pp.242-251
28. Quoted in ibidem, p.243

## Chapter 2

29. J. A. Rogers, *World's Great Men of Color: Volume 1*, US, Macmillan, 1972, p.67
30. Quoted in ibidem, p.71
31. Quoted in ibidem
32. Quoted in ibidem, p.70
33. Ibidem, p.72
34. Quoted in ibidem, p.70
35. Quoted in ibidem, pp.68-9
36. W. E. B. Du Bois, *The World and Africa*, US, International Publishers, 1965, p.190, Janheinz Jahn, *Neo-African Literature*, US, Grove Press, 1968, p.28, and J. A. Rogers, *World's Great Men of Color: Volume 1*, p.142
37. Runoko Rashidi, *African Star Over Asia*, UK, Books of Africa, 2012, pp.172-3
38. Janheinz Jahn, *Neo-African Literature*, p.26
39. W. E. B. Du Bois, *The World and Africa*, p.190
40. Charles Dudley Warmer, *Library of the World's Best Literature: Volume 2*, at http://www.gutenberg.org/files/12788/12788-h/12788-h.htm#A_FAIR_LADY
41. Quoted in Janheinz Jahn, *Neo-African Literature*, p.26
42. Ibidem, pp.28-29
43. Quoted in ibidem, p.29
44. Quoted in ibidem, pp.29-30
45. J. A. Rogers, *World's Great Men of Color: Volume 1*, p.163
46. Jim Al-Khalili, *Science: Islam's forgotten geniuses*, in *The Telegraph*, 29 January 2008
47. J. A. Rogers, *World's Great Men of Color: Volume 1*, p.164

## Chapter 3

48. Cf. David Buxton, *The Abyssinians*, UK, Thames and Hudson, 1970, p.119

# Early Black Literature

49. Ibidem
50. Peter Garlake, *Early Art and Architecture of Africa*, UK, Oxford University Press, 2002, p.76
51. Roderick Grierson, *Dreaming of Jerusalem*, in *African Zion*, ed Roderick Grierson, US, InterCultura, 1993, p.7
52. Teddesse Tamrat, *Church and State in Ethiopia: The Early Centuries*, in *African Zion*, ed Roderick Grierson, US, InterCultura, 1993, pp.33-4
53. Anu M'Bantu & Fari Supiya, *Ethiopia's First Christian Emperor: Ezana of Axum*, in *West Africa*, Issue 4303, p.43
54. Martin Bailey, *Discovery of earliest illuminated manuscript*, in *The Art Newspaper*, No.214, June 2010. See internet at http://ethiopianheritagefund.org/artsNewspaper.html
55. Dr Richard Pankhurst, *A Serious Question of Ethiopian Studies: Five Thousand Ethiopian Manuscripts Abroad and the International Community*, at http://theblacklistpub.ning.com/group/theblacklistview/forum/topics/a-serious-question-of
56. David Buxton, *The Abyssinians*, p.120
57. Getatchew Haile, *Ethiopic Literature*, in *African Zion*, ed Roderick Grierson, US, InterCultura, 1993, pp.47-8
58. David Buxton, *The Abyssinians*, p.122
59. Ibidem, pp.123-9
60. Ibidem, pp.126-9
61. Ibidem, pp.123-4
62. Ibidem, p.124
63. Ibidem, pp.125-6
64. Ibidem, p.124 and Getatchew Haile, *Ethiopic Literature*, in *African Zion*, pp.49-50
65. David Buxton, *The Abyssinians*, p.130
66. Getatchew Haile, *Ethiopic Literature*, in *African Zion*, pp.48, 51
67. David Buxton, *The Abyssinians*, pp.131-2
68. Ibidem, pp.129-30, 134
69. Ibidem, p.134
70. Otto Neugebauer, *Ethiopic Astronomy and Computus*, Germany, Osterreiche Akademie Der Wissenschaften, 1979, pp.20, 91, 95, 99, 107-108, 183-184, 198, 200-201, 232-233
71. Richard Pankhurst, *An Introduction to the Medical History of Ethiopia*, US, Red Sea Press, 1990, pp.26-30, 75-80, 93-101, 104-111, 113-136

## Chapter 4

72. Derek A. Welsby, *The Medieval Kingdoms of Nubia*, UK, The British Museum Press, 2002, pp.237-8

73. R. Sean O'Fahey, *Arabic literature in the eastern half of Africa*, in *The Meanings of Timbuktu*, ed Shamil Jeppe and Souleymane Bachir Diagne, South Africa, HSRC, 2008, p.333
74. Ibidem, pp.333-4

## Chapter 5

75. Murray Last, *The book in the Sokoto Caliphate*, in *The Meanings of Timbuktu*, ed Shamil Jeppe and Souleymane Bachir Diagne, South Africa, HSRC, 2008, pp.137, 140
76. Quoted in Sir Richmond Palmer, *The Bornu Sahara and Sudan*, UK, John Murray, 1936, frontispiece
77. Y. B. Usman, *The Birne of Katsina*, in *Cities of the Savannah*, ed Garba Ashiwaju, Nigeria, The Nigeria Magazine, no date given, p.41
78. Claudia Zaslavsky, *Africa Counts*, US, Lawrence Hill & Co., 1973, pp.138-151
79. Cited by Hamid Bobboyi, *Ajami literature and the study of the Sokoto Caliphate*, in *The Meanings of Timbuktu*, ed Shamil Jeppe and Souleymane Bachir Diagne, South Africa, HSRC, 2008, p.123
80. Ibidem, p.124
81. Murray Last, *The book in the Sokoto Caliphate*, in *The Meanings of Timbuktu*, p.144
82. Hamid Bobboyi, *Ajami literature and the study of the Sokoto Caliphate*, in *The Meanings of Timbuktu*, pp.125-7
83. Beverly B. Mack, *Muslim women scholars in the nineteenth and twentieth centuries: Morocco to Nigeria*, in *The Meanings of Timbuktu*, ed Shamil Jeppe and Souleymane Bachir Diagne, South Africa, HSRC, 2008, p.169
84. Ibidem, pp.169-171
85. Janheinz Jahn, *Neo-African Literature*, US, Grove Press, 1968, pp.73-7
86. Murray Last, *The book in the Sokoto Caliphate*, in *The Meanings of Timbuktu*, p.145
87. Quoted in Janheinz Jahn, *Neo-African Literature*, p.74

## Chapter 6

88. R. Sean O'Fahey, *Arabic literature in the eastern half of Africa*, in *The Meanings of Timbuktu*, ed Shamil Jeppe and Souleymane Bachir Diagne, South Africa, HSRC, 2008, pp.334, 335
89. Ibidem, p.334
90. R. Sean O'Fahey, *Arabic literature in the eastern half of Africa*, in *The Meanings of Timbuktu*, ed Shamil Jeppe and Souleymane Bachir Diagne, South Africa, HSRC, 2008, pp.335, 343
91. Kitula King'ei, *Historical And Folkloric Elements In Fumo Liyongo's Epic*, 2001, at http://www.folklore.ee/folklore/vol16/liyongo.pdf

# Early Black Literature

92. Quoted in ibidem
93. R. Sean O'Fahey, *Arabic literature in the eastern half of Africa,* in *The Meanings of Timbuktu,* p.335
94. Ibidem, p.343
95. *Swahili poetry,* at http://www.snipview.com/q/Swahili%20poetry
96. Quoted in Kitula King'ei, *Historical And Folkloric Elements In Fumo Liyongo's Epic*
97. R. Sean O'Fahey, *Arabic literature in the eastern half of Africa,* in *The Meanings of Timbuktu,* p.344
98. Anne K. Bang, *Textual sources on an Islamic African Past: Arabic material in Zazibar's National Archive,* in *The Meanings of Timbuktu,* ed Shamil Jeppe and Souleymane Bachir Diagne, South Africa, HSRC, 2008, pp.356-7

## Chapter 7

99. Arthur P. Davis, J. Saunders Redding and Joyce Ann Joyce, *Selected African American Writing from 1760 to 1910,* US, Bantam Books, 1991, pp.4-5 and *Bars Fight by Lucy Terry,* at http://www.berfrois.com/2011/12/bars-fight-lucy-terry/
100. *Bars Fight by Lucy Terry,* at http://www.berfrois.com/2011/12/bars-fight-lucy-terry/
101. Arthur P. Davis, J. Saunders Redding and Joyce Ann Joyce, *Selected African American Writing from 1760 to 1910,* pp.11-15 and Janheinz Jahn, *Neo-African Literature,* US, Grove Press, 1968, pp.36-7.
102. *Phillis Wheatley,* at http://en.wikipedia.org/wiki/Phillis_Wheatley
103. Arthur P. Davis, J. Saunders Redding and Joyce Ann Joyce, *Selected African American Writing from 1760 to 1910,* pp.16-17
104. *slave narrative,* at http://en.wikipedia.org/wiki/Slave_narrative
105. *William Wells Brown,* at http://en.wikipedia.org/wiki/William_Wells_Brown
106. Janheinz Jahn, *Neo-African Literature,* p.131 and Arthur P. Davis, J. Saunders Redding and Joyce Ann Joyce, *Selected African American Writing from 1760 to 1910,* pp.198-9
107. *Frances Harper,* at http://en.wikipedia.org/wiki/Frances_Harper and Arthur P. Davis, J. Saunders Redding and Joyce Ann Joyce, *Selected African American Writing from 1760 to 1910,* pp.16-17
108. Quoted in *Arthur Schomburg, Racial Integrity: A Plea for the Establishment of a Chair of Negro History in our Schools and Colleges, etc,* US, Black Classic Press reprint, 1913, pp.10-11
109. *Frank J. Webb,* at http://en.wikipedia.org/wiki/Frank_J._Webb
110. Janheinz Jahn, *Neo-African Literature,* pp.149-50

**WHEN WE RULED**
**Second Edition**

ROBIN WALKER

Available from www.whenweruled.com

# PART THREE

## THE AUTHOR

# ROBIN WALKER

## Biography

Robin Walker 'The Black History Man' was born in London but has also lived in Jamaica. He attended the London School of Economics and Political Science where he read Economics.

In 1991 and 1992, he studied African World Studies with the brilliant Dr Femi Biko and later with Mr Kenny Bakie. Between 1993 and 1994, he trained as a secondary school teacher at Edge Hill College (linked to the University of Lancaster).

Since 1992 and up to the present period, Robin Walker has lectured in adult education, taught university short courses, and chaired conferences in African World Studies, Egyptology and Black History. The venues have been in Toxteth (Liverpool), Manchester, Leeds, Bradford, Huddersfield, Birmingham, Cambridge, Buckinghamshire and London.

Since 1994 he has taught Economics, Business & Finance, Mathematics, Information Communications Technology, PSHE/Citizenship and also History at various schools in London and Essex.

In 1999 he wrote *Classical Splendour: Roots of Black History* published in the UK by Bogle L'Ouverture Publications. In the same year, he co-authored (with Siaf Millar) *The West African Empire of Songhai,* a textbook used by many schools across the country.

In 2000 he co-authored (again with Siaf Millar) *Sword, Seal and Koran,* another book on the Songhai Empire of West Africa.

In 2006 he wrote the seminal *When We Ruled.* This was the most advanced synthesis on Ancient and Mediaeval African history ever written by a single author. It was a massive expansion of his earlier book *Classical Splendour: Roots of Black History* and established his reputation as the leading Black History educational service provider.

In 2008 he wrote *Before The Slave Trade,* a highly pictorial companion volume to *When We Ruled.*

Between 2011 and 2014 he wrote a series of e-books for download sold through Amazon Kindle. These e-books covered history, business, religion, music, and science.

In 2013 he co-authored (with Siaf Millar and Saran Keita) *Everyday Life In An Early West African Empire*. It was a massive expansion on the earlier book *Sword, Seal & Koran*. He updated *When We Ruled* by incorporating nearly all the images from *Before The Slave Trade*. He also wrote a trilogy of books entitled *Blacks and Science Volumes One, Two* and *Three*.

In 2014 he wrote *The Rise and Fall of Black Wall Street and the Seven Key Empowerment Principles, Blacks and Religion Volume One*, and *If You Want to Learn Early African History START HERE*. He also co-authored (with John Matthews) *African Mathematics: History, Textbook and Classroom Lessons*.

In 2015 he wrote the book that you are holding right now.

### Speaking Engagements

Looking for a speaker for your next event?

The author Robin Walker 'The Black History Man' is dynamic and engaging, both as a speaker and a workshop leader. He brings Black or African history alive, making it relevant for the present generation. You will love his perfect blend of accessibility, engagement, and academic rigour where learning becomes fun.

Walker is available to give speaking engagements to a variety of audiences. One of his most popular lectures is *Roots of Black Music*. Another relevant lecture is *Roots of Black Literature*.

To book Robin Walker for your next event, send an email to historicalwalker@yahoo.com

# The Author

**If you want to learn Early African History START HERE**

*Robin Walker*

Available from www.amazon.com

# AFRICAN MATHEMATICS
## History, Textbook and Classroom Lessons

**Robin Walker & John Matthews**

Available from www.amazon.com

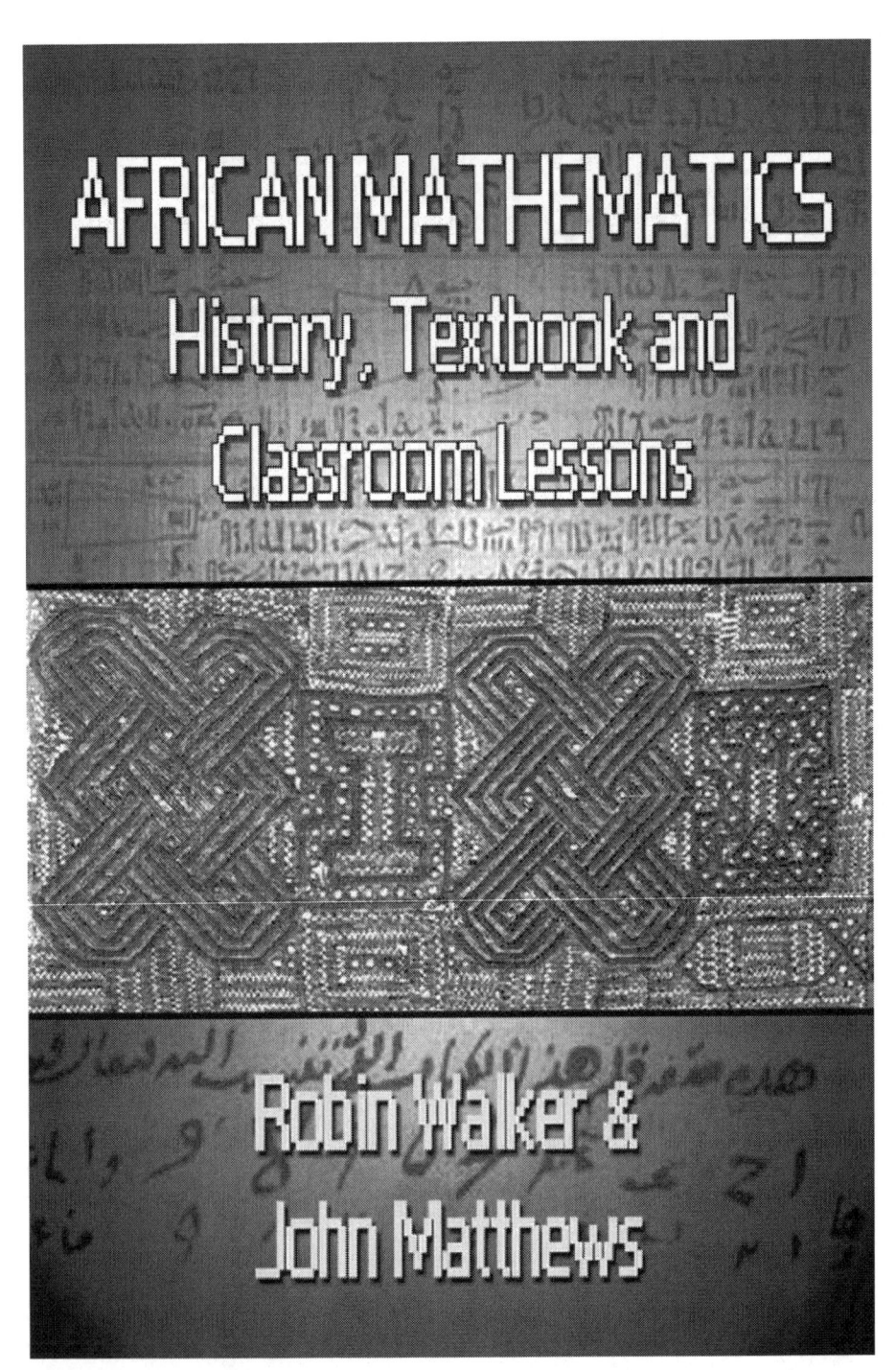

# INDEX

Adams, Hunter 10-14
*Admonitions of Ipuwer* 51-52
African American literature 74-84
African American music 21-40
Aitken, Laurel 35
Allen, Richard 23
Al Jahiz 57-58
Al Maghili 67
Antar 56-57
Arabian literature 54-58
Armstrong, Louis 25, 28-29
Art Blakey and the Jazz Messengers 32
Asma'u, Nana 69
Atkins, Juan 38, 39
*Azan, The* 19

Bambaataa, Afrika 38
*Bars Fight* 74
Basie, Count 29
Bauza, Mario 29
Ben-Jochannan, Yosef 49
Berry, Chuck 33
Big Band 29
Bilal 19
Black Codes 21, 29
Blake, Eubie 27
Blues, The 16, 24, 25
Bobboyi, Hamid 68
Bolden, Buddy 27-28
*Book of Animals* 57-58
Brass Band 24-25
Brown, James 33-34, 35-36
Brown, William Wells 77-78
Buster, Prince 35
Buxton, David 59, 61, 63

Calls and Cries 21-22
Calypso 31, 34
Charles, Ray 33, 34

*Chrismus On The Plantation* 83
Classical music, African 15-19
Clinton, George 36
Cole, Stranger 35
Conley, Arthur 33
Cooke, Sam 33
Cruz, Celia 29
Cuban music 29-30

Dalby, Winifred 16
Davidson, Basil 8-9, 68
Davis, Miles 31-32
*Deggwa* 16
Diagne, Souleymane Bachir 47-48
Diddley, Bo 33
Disco 36
Domino, Fats 33
Dorsey, Thomas 23
Du Bois, W. E. B. 56
Dunbar, Paul Lawrence 82-84

Earth, Wind and Fire 36
Egyptian literature 49-53
Egyptian music 8-14, 22
Elhadj, Salem Ould 18
Ellis, Alton 35
Engel, Carl 9, 17
Erman, Adolf 53
Ethiopian literature 59-64
Ethiopian music 14, 15-16

*Fables* 55, 56
Fellasha chants 15-16
Fisk University Jubilee Singers 23, 24
Fitzgerald, Ella 29
Flash, Grandmaster 38
Franklin, Aretha 33-34
*Fumo Liongo* 71-72
Funk 36

# Index

Funk, Farley 'Jackmaster' 36

Gamble, Kenny 36-37
Garlake, Peter 59-61
Gillespie, Dizzy 30
Golden Ode 57
Gospel music 23
*Gospels of Abba Garima* 60, 61
Gottheil, Richard 56
*Great Hymn to Aten* 53
Grierson, Roderick 61
Grime music 39
*Gunda Gunde Gospels* 62

Hammon, Briton 76, 77
Handy, William Christopher 24
Harold Melvin and the Blue Notes 36
Harper, Frances Ellen Watkins 78-80
Henderson, Fletcher 29
Highlife 20
Hip Hop 37-38
House music 38-39
Huff, Leon 36-37
Hurley, Steve 'Silk' 36

*Instruction of Amenemope* 49-51
Isley Brothers 34

Jahn, Janheinz 47, 56, 57, 69-70
Jamaican music 34-36
Jazz 24, 27-32
Jefferson, Marshall 38-39
Jegede, Tunde 19
Jeppe, Shamil 47-48
Jimmy Smith Trio 32
Jobson, Richard 16-18
John Coltrane Quartet 32
Joplin, Scott 27
Jungle 39

Kati, Mahmud 19
Kebede, Ashenafi 5, 10, 16
Kitchener, Lord 344
Knuckles, Frankie 38
Konte family 19
Kool and the Gang 36
Kool Herc, DJ 37

Last, Murray 67, 69
LL Cool J 38
Lockman 54-56
Lover's Rock 39
Lunceford, Jimmie 29

Machito, Franz 29, 30
Malian music 16-19
Mambo 29
Marcel, J. J. 54
Mardi Gras 25
Marley, Bob 36
Marsalis, Wynton 39-40
Martha Reeves and the Vandellas 33
May, Derrick 38, 39
Mbaqanga 20
*Miracles of St Menas* 65
Modern Jazz 31-32
Modern Jazz Quartet 32
Monk, Thelonius 31
Morton, Jelly Roll 28
Motown 33
Muhumutapan music 19
Murray, Albert 5
Music defined 7

Neugebauer, Otto 64
Nketia, J. H. Kwabena 19
North African music 19-20
NWA 39

Obenga, Théophile 14, 53
*Ode to Ethiopia* 83-84
O'Fahey, R. Sean 65, 71
O Jays, The 36
*On being brought from Africa to America* 77
*On the Obligations of Princes* 67
Oriental music 19-20
Ornette Coleman Quartet 32

Pankhurst, Richard 61, 64
Parker, Charlie 31
Phillips, John 68
Pickett, Wilson 33
*Poems on Various Subjects* 75
Polyrhythmic Dance music 20
Popular music, African 15, 20

# Index

Public Enemy 38
Pythagoras 10

Ragtime 27
Rainey, Ma 24
Rashidi, Runoko 56
Redding, Otis 33
Reggae 35-36
Richard, Little 33
Rockabilly 33
Rock and Roll 33
Rogers, J. A. 54, 56
Run DMC 38

Saharan music 8-9
Sam & Dave 33
Saunderson, Kevin 38, 39
Savary, Claude-Étienne 54
Schomburg, Arthur 47, 79-80
Scott, James 27
Sea shanty 22-23
Senwosret III, *Praise Song* 52-53
Ska 34-35
Smith, Bessie 26
Smokey Robinson and the Miracles 33
Soca 39
Songhai Empire music 19
Soul music 24, 33-36
Spirituals 22
Stone, Sly 36
Sudanese literature 65-66
Summer, Donna 36
Supremes, The 33
Swahili literature 71-73
Swing 29

Techno 38-39
Temptations, The 33
*The Garies and Their Friends* 80-81
*The Slave Auction* 79
*The Soul's Awakening* 73
Three Degrees, The 36
Toots and the Maytals 35-36
Traditional music, African 15
Turner, Ike 33

U-Roy 36
Uthman Dan Fodio 68-69

Velikovsky, Immanuel 51-52

Webb, Chick 29
Webb, Frank J. 80-81
Wheatley, Phillis 74-77
White, Barry 36
Wilson, Amos 1
Work Song 22-23

Yam Festival 25
Yared, St 16
Youth, Big 36
Young, Lester 29

Ziryab 20

# Everyday Life in an early West African Empire

A Jacinth Martin Publication

Afterword by Runoko Rashidi

## Written By Robin Walker
## Siaf Millar & Saran Keita

Available from www.everydaylifeinanearlywestafricanempire.com

Made in the USA
Charleston, SC
20 March 2015